# EFFORTLESSLY
# ELEVATED Eats

# EFFORTLESSLY ELEVATED *Eats*

## Unique, Flavorful Recipes for EVERYDAY COOKING

**JENNY HURLEY**

creator of SUNNY WITH SHADOWS

PAGE STREET
PUBLISHING CO.

PAGE STREET
PUBLISHING CO.

First published in 2023 by
Page Street Publishing Co.
27 Congress Street, Suite 1511
Salem, MA 01970
www.pagestreetpublishing.com

Distributed by Macmillan, sales in Canada by The Canadian Manda Group.

27   26   25   24   23     1   2   3   4   5

ISBN-13: 978-1-64567-925-7
ISBN-10: 1-64567-925-7

Library of Congress Control Number: 2022950869

Cover and book design by Laura Benton for Page Street Publishing Co.
Photography by Jenny Hurley

Printed and bound in the United States

**I want to dedicate this book to my family.
Without them, this book wouldn't exist.**

# Contents

# Introduction

I stumbled upon a short video of Julia Child on Instagram the other day. *Yes, Julia, exactly*, is what I thought while watching, because she hit the nail right on the head. My exact thoughts, word for word.

She said, "You know, one thing I think a lot of people are just so scared of is any recipe they see that says sugar, syrup or caramel, they go, '*Ohhh* [classic Julia], I won't try anything like that.' And that is this awful American syndrome of *fear of failure*. If you're going to have a sense of fear of failure you're just never going to learn how to cook, because cooking is just one failure after another, which is how you finally learn. You've got to develop what the French call *je–m'en-foutisme*, or 'I don't care what happens.' The sky can fall, omelets can go all over the stove, I'm going to learn, I shall overcome! If you're not going to be ready to fail, you're not going to learn how to cook."

A lot of the recipes in this book will sound intimidating and you might think, *I don't know if I can do that*. Well, let me just go ahead and tell you, *you can*. If I can do it, you can. I am a self-taught home cook who learned to cook by doing, and you know what else I learned? Cooking is easy if you aren't afraid to fail. You have to just start doing and stop worrying what may or may not happen. I used to spend most of my time reading recipes and saying, "Oh, that sounds hard," or "This seems really intense," but then one day, I just read through a recipe and started cooking. Since then, I have learned how to make my own pasta (all shapes and sizes), roast garlic on a daily basis, cure egg yolks (so easy), make a roux (seriously, it's just butter and flour—why was I always so scared of this?), make caramel in every consistency you can think of (hard candy, sauce, toffee) and much, much more. Sometimes I fail (I'm lookin' at you, caramel), but that's okay. Learn from your mistakes and *that* is how you learn to cook.

My main focus for this cookbook is how to easily elevate a dish at home. By this, I mean just taking a recipe that is *ordinary* and making it *extraordinary* by elevating the ingredients. Cooking really begins with the ingredients you choose. Depending on what you have to work with, the meal can be very different. This doesn't always mean it has to be more expensive. By choosing to start with roasted garlic instead of raw garlic, for example, all you've done is taken an ordinary ingredient and made it more extraordinary in flavor. I'm all for pot roast, but let's roast it in wine and top it with handmade biscuits, ya know?

Sometimes, it requires patience, such as how it takes two weeks to cure egg yolks. Raw garlic and roasted garlic cost the exact same amount of money, but roasted garlic costs more time. The thing about food is you can generally find something delicious at every price range; you just need to know how to put those ingredients together.

If you take anything away from this cookbook, I hope it is that you can make restaurant-quality dishes at home. They use the same ingredients you can buy at the store; they just put a little bit more care, effort and creativity into them, and you can, too. Now, let's get cooking!

# ELEVATED INGREDIENTS
## (and their substitutions if they have them)

This chapter is the reason I wrote this cookbook. I started adding these simple ingredients to my dishes and suddenly realized that having restaurant-quality food at home was not unattainable. It wasn't even hard! Through working with these ingredients, I learned that a little creativity and care will make all the difference in how delicious your food ends up being, and not a single one of them is difficult to make or use. Some take a little bit of time, but that time is well worth the outcome, trust me; and some, you just buy! How easy is that? All these elevated ingredients will be used throughout my entire cookbook, and I hope that you can come away from this book with a better understanding of them to explore in your own ways every day!

*This is probably my favorite and most used ingredient on the list. I've always had an immense love for garlic, ever since I was little. Of course, once I figured out that you can roast it to make a completely different flavor, I was hooked. Roasted garlic becomes much milder, so you can use more of it. You get the garlic flavor, with a hint of sweetness and a lot less of the rawness fresh garlic brings.*

# ROASTED GARLIC

1 garlic head
1 tbsp (15 ml) olive oil
Salt and freshly ground black pepper

### How to roast garlic in an oven

Preheat the oven to 400°F (200°C). Slice the top off the entire garlic head and remove any excess skin. Place the garlic head upright on a sheet of aluminum foil, drizzle the oil over the top and sprinkle with salt and pepper to taste. Wrap tightly with foil and bake for 40 minutes.

### How to roast garlic in an air fryer

Preheat an air fryer to 350°F (180°C). Slice the top off the entire garlic head and remove any excess skin. Place the garlic head upright on a sheet of aluminum foil, drizzle the oil over each top and sprinkle with salt and pepper. Wrap tightly with foil and bake for 20 minutes.

## RECIPES THAT USE ROASTED GARLIC

**Easy Roasted Garlic Tomato Galette Made Sweet and Tangy with Balsamic Reduction (page 55)**

**Loaded Potato and Leek Soup Elevated with Smoky Cheddar, Crispy Pancetta and Crème Fraîche (page 56)**

**Quick Full-Flavor Cheesy Grits Elevated with Roasted Garlic (page 93)**

**Everyday Buttermilk Drop Biscuits with Cheddar and Roasted Garlic (page 86)**

**Note**

1 *If you are making any of the recipes in this cookbook, you don't want to replace the roasted garlic with anything else. Raw garlic will be too powerful and change the dish completely. Take the extra time and roast the garlic; you won't be sorry!*

*Miso paste is my favorite newfound elevated ingredient, and you don't even have to make it! You can find miso paste at any Asian market, but I mainly get mine from Amazon and it comes right to my door. Doesn't get much easier than that! The flavor it adds to a dish is incomparable to any other ingredient. It's a paste made from fermented soybeans that is mixed with salt and koji (a mold also used to make sake). There are a lot of different types of miso paste, but I mainly use brown miso paste in this cookbook. Brown miso paste is aged longer, so it has a saltier and more pronounced flavor than white miso paste. That's why I like it, and you will, too!*

# MISO PASTE

1 tub brown miso paste

**Note**

1- *There really isn't anything you can replace miso paste with, but you can always add more salt to a dish if you are missing the miso. The dish will still taste different, but miso paste adds a large amount of umami and salt flavor, so adding a little more salt could help get you there.*

*This is probably the second-easiest elevated ingredient to make. All you really need is balsamic vinegar. Boiling it down and reducing it takes away most of the bite that it has when it is just vinegar, and of course, adding brown sugar gives it even more sweetness. This is the perfect, sweet complement to your savory dishes or to drizzle on almost anything (I've even eaten it with ice cream).*

# BALSAMIC REDUCTION

1 cup (240 ml) balsamic vinegar

1 tbsp (15 g) brown sugar

In a small saucepan, combine the balsamic vinegar and brown sugar. Bring to a boil over medium-high heat and then lower the heat and simmer for another 10 to 15 minutes, or until the liquid reduces by half. It should be able to coat the back of a spoon. Pour into an airtight glass jar, allow to cool to room temperature and then store in the fridge for up to 3 months. I like to keep a jar of this in my fridge at all times because it is good on so many different things!

## RECIPES THAT USE BALSAMIC REDUCTION

Easy Roasted Garlic Tomato Galette Made Sweet and Tangy with Balsamic Reduction (page 55)

Marinated Pork Tenderloin with Apple Chutney Made Sweet and Tangy with Balsamic Reduction (page 35)

**Substitution**

1- *You can buy this already bottled if you want to have it on hand without needing to worry about making it. There are a ton of brands out there, from your basic grocery store house brand to Bertolli®, that make a super delicious balsamic glaze sauce! However, I always suggest you make this reduction from scratch if you have the time, as it is so easy.*

*Now, this is probably an ingredient you may have never heard of before, so I am excited to introduce you to it! Curing egg yolks may seem a little odd for some, but it is a cooking method that dates back to fifth-century China. It takes extra time (literally, just a waiting game), but with very little hands-on time. You can cure a dozen yolks at a time and keep them in your fridge for up to a month. They add a salty umami pop, unlike anything else I've ever tasted, to anything they are grated onto. They are also a great Parmesan cheese substitution for those who are lactose-intolerant!*

# CURED EGG YOLKS

2 cups (270 g) kosher salt, divided

10 large eggs

Pour 1 cup (135 g) of the kosher salt evenly into a 9 x 13-inch (23 x 33-cm) glass or ceramic baking dish. Using an egg or the back of a spoon, make 10 indentions in the salt, each large enough for an egg yolk to sit in. Once you've made all the indentions, carefully crack the eggs and place an unbroken yolk in each indention (save the whites for other recipes, such as meringue or pavlovas). Gently cover the yolks with the remaining cup (135 g) of salt. Place the dish in the refrigerator for 5 days.

After 5 days, break through the salt to remove the yolks. At this stage, they will be solid but a little sticky. The salt coagulates the yolk to make it solid, but the drying time will finish off that process. Go ahead and rinse any remaining salt off them so they are clean.

Now, lay them equally distanced apart along a skinny piece of cheesecloth (approximately 6 x 20 inches [15 x 51 cm] or so). Fold the cheesecloth over twice widthwise to enclose the yolks in a long tube, and then tie a piece of kitchen string between each yolk. Hang in a dry, cool place for 1 week. I hung mine in a closet. At the end of the week, all you have to do is unwrap the yolks and store in an airtight container in the fridge for up to a month!

**RECIPES THAT USE CURED EGG YOLKS**

**Simple Summer Fettuccine Made Restaurant Worthy with Cherry Tomato Garlic Confit Sauce (page 25)**

**Brussels Sprouts Salad with Roasted Red Pepper Aioli and Parmesan Crisps (page 94)**

**Classic Wedge Salad with Blue Cheese Dressing and Cured Egg Yolk (page 98)**

**Substitutions**

1- *When any of the recipes in this cookbook calls for cured egg yolk, it can be replaced with Parmesan cheese. The cured egg yolks provide the same salty, slightly cheesy aspect that complements pasta and salads.*

*This is my favorite spice blend and you will see it in a lot of my dessert recipes. It is incredibly easy to make; you just have to mix a couple of spices together and you're done! Mine contains cinnamon, ginger, cardamom, nutmeg and cloves. I like to mix up a big batch and keep it in a glass Mason jar so I always have it on hand.*

# CHAI SPICE MIX

1/4 cup (31 g) ground cinnamon
2 tbsp (11 g) ground ginger
4 tsp (8 g) ground cardamom
1/2 tsp ground nutmeg
1/2 tsp ground cloves

In a bowl, mix the cinnamon, ginger, cardamom, nutmeg and cloves together and store in an airtight container. This recipe makes about 1/2 cup (49 g).

### RECIPES THAT USE CHAI SPICE MIX

**Best Ever Apple Upside-Down Cake with Buttermilk and Chai Spice (page 126)**

**Maple Coffee Cake Elevated with Crème Fraîche (page 129)**

**Approachable Mini Cinnamon Pavlovas Elevated with Brown Butter Caramelized Apples (page 111)**

### Substitution

1- *For the recipes in this cookbook that call for chai spice mix, you can always substitute just cinnamon. However, you will be missing a huge depth of flavor without the other spices involved in the chai spice blend.*

*When I discovered crème fraîche, I fell in love. I thought, What is this magic? It tastes like a cross between sour cream and cream cheese, both of which I also love, but it is even more than that. It is extremely versatile, and you can use it alone or add so many different ingredients to it to create a whole new flavor profile.*

# CRÈME FRAÎCHE

1 (8-oz [237-ml]) tub crème fraîche

### Substitution

1– *In most of the recipes in this cookbook that call for crème fraîche, it can be replaced with sour cream, which gives the same coolness, creaminess and texture as crème fraîche, so it is comparable. However, if you can, I urge you to use crème fraîche because of the added richness and depth that sour cream is sadly missing.*

## RECIPES THAT USE CRÈME FRAÎCHE

Bougie Baked Mac and Cheese Made Next Level with Gruyère and Crème Fraîche (page 89)

Brussels Sprouts Salad with Roasted Red Pepper Aioli and Parmesan Crisps (page 94)

Everyday Chipotle Tofu Burrito Bowls with Lime Crème Fraîche Crema (page 36)

Garlic Shrimp Linguine Elevated with Creamy Crème Fraîche White Wine Sauce (page 26)

Next Level Cheese Steak Fries with Smoky Cheddar Crème Fraîche Cheese Sauce (page 76)

Maple Coffee Cake Elevated with Crème Fraîche (page 129)

*Browned butter adds a completely different dimension to a dish, almost effortlessly. Browning the butter means the milk solids sink to the bottom and separate from the fat, causing the butter to take on a divine nuttiness to it. It's almost unexplainable, you really need to just try it out for yourself and you will not be sorry.*

# BROWNED BUTTER

½ cup (114 g) unsalted butter

This is incredibly easy; you just have to be patient and watchful. In a small saucepan over medium-low heat, place however much butter your recipe calls for. Melt the butter slowly. It will go through a couple of different stages before it starts to brown, taking about 10 minutes total.

First, it will melt as usual, then it will be slightly foamy and white. You need to stir and watch it at this point, because once the milk solids start to sink to the bottom (they will be white at first), that is when things really start to happen. You will see a bunch of white flakes at the bottom of the saucepan when you stir, and those are what is going to brown. It happens really quickly once it starts to turn golden, so watch carefully until the specks are a nice, rich golden brown and then quickly remove them from the heat and pour into a glass or ceramic bowl. If using in a recipe that calls for eggs, you need to cool down the butter first to prevent cooking the eggs, so just keep in mind what you are using this for!

## RECIPES THAT USE BROWN BUTTER

Pumpkin Pasta with Andouille Sausage Made Special with Crème Fraîche and Brown Butter Walnut Sage Crumble (page 29)

Simple Apple Hand Pies with Brown Butter Apples and Chunks of Brie (page 107)

Epic Small-Batch Chocolate Chip Cookies Made Bakery Worthy with Miso Brown Butter (page 108)

Easiest Ever Blue Cheese Pear Galette with Brown Butter Sage Walnut Crumble (page 133)

*Garlic confit is a beautiful, beautiful thing. You basically tenderize garlic (and can also add cherry tomatoes and shallots) by cooking it low and slow in olive or avocado oil until it becomes soft and spreadable. This also leaves you with a bunch of garlic-infused olive or avocado oil, which is never a bad thing. This can go in and on so many things, really too many to even list. Of all the elevated ingredients discussed in this section, I want to encourage you to experiment with this one the most.*

# GARLIC CONFIT

1¹/₂ cups (360 g) cloves garlic, peeled
¹/₂ tsp coarse sea salt
¹/₄ tsp freshly ground black pepper
1 to 1¹/₂ cups (240 to 360 ml) olive or avocado oil
2 sprigs rosemary
2 sprigs thyme

Preheat the oven to 250°F (120°C). Arrange the garlic in a single layer in a small baking dish (I used a 2-cup [475-ml] mini Dutch oven). Sprinkle with the salt and pepper and then pour the oil on top to coat. Place the rosemary and thyme on top and then bake for 1¹/₂ to 2 hours, or until all the cloves are tender.

Store in a Mason jar *in the fridge* (very important) for no longer than 3 weeks. I like to do small batches so I don't have to worry about using it up quickly. I love dipping crusty bread into the confit, and you can use the garlic-infused oil in any and every dish you need oil for!

*See photo on page 10.

## RECIPES THAT USE GARLIC CONFIT

**Simple Summer Fettuccine Made Restaurant Worthy with Cherry Tomato Garlic Confit Sauce (page 25)**

**Effortless Garlic Confit Feta Dip Packed with Herbs and Sun-Dried Tomatoes (page 75)**

**Southern Comfort Gouda Grit Cakes Topped with Cherry Tomato Garlic Confit (page 78)**

### Substitutions

1– *Roasted garlic plus olive or avocado oil would be the closest substitution for garlic confit.*

# EASY, EXCEPTIONAL ENTRÉES

You don't always have to go to a fancy restaurant to get fancy food. Honestly, most of the time I go out to eat, I just end up disappointed and a little poorer. These entrées, which you can make right in the comfort of your very own home, are fancy yet approachable. They are totally doable and also totally delicious. Whether it's just making something for you to have for dinner on a Tuesday night, such as the Quick and Easy Umami Tofu Bowl Made Restaurant Worthy with Sticky Dijon Soy Maple Sauce (page 48), or you are having guests over and you want to impress them with the Elevated Red Wine and Dark Chocolate Pot Roast with Homemade Mini Biscuit Topping (page 32), there is something in this chapter that you can rely on. Full-flavor dinners aren't just for restaurants anymore, so save yourself money and make one of these mouthwatering dinners at home. Plus, you can cook in your sweatpants while watching your favorite TV show; I mean, does it get any better than that?

*If you dog-ear any recipe in this cookbook, it should be this one. The time for this dish is almost completely hands-off, and you get a bonus recipe in the most delicious tomato, garlic and shallot confit, which elevates the dish and leaves you with a jar full of infused avocado oil that you can use for a ton of other things. The burrata adds an additional layer of complexity. The rest of this dish comes together in a flash and the ingredients turn this what could be just an average pasta dish into a complex-tasting one fit for a queen!*

# SIMPLE SUMMER FETTUCCINE

Made Restaurant Worthy with Cherry Tomato Garlic Confit Sauce

**Prep time: 10 minutes** · **Cook time: 1 hour 15 minutes** · **Servings: 4**

### Confit

1½ lb (680 g) cherry tomatoes

3 heads garlic

2 shallots

2 cups (480 ml) olive or avocado oil

### Roasted Vine Tomatoes

3 stems' worth of cherry tomatoes still on vine (about 12 oz [340 g])

2 tbsp (30 ml) olive oil

Salt and freshly ground black pepper

### Pasta

1 lb (450 g) dried fettuccine

Zest of 1 lemon

1 tbsp (15 ml) fresh lemon juice

8 oz (225 g) burrata

1 cured egg yolk (see page 16)

First things first: Get your confit going! For how to make garlic confit, see page 21. This recipe calls for a cherry tomato, garlic and shallot confit, so you are going to follow the steps for the garlic confit but use a larger ovenproof dish and add the cherry tomatoes and shallots. When your confit is done, remove it from the oven and let it cool. Leave the oven on.

Roast the tomatoes: On a baking sheet, arrange the cherry tomatoes, leaving the vines on, and coat them with the olive oil. Season with salt and pepper. Bake for 15 to 20 minutes or until the tomatoes start to burst. Remove them from the oven and set aside to top the pasta once it's done. Keep the oven on for the final steps!

Once you're ready to make your pasta, return to the confit. Drain the oil from the tomatoes, garlic and shallots and transfer it to an airtight glass container. Set the tomatoes, garlic and shallots aside. Cook the fettuccine according to the package instructions.

While the pasta cooks, pour ¼ cup (60 ml) of the confit oil into a large, ovenproof skillet. Add the cherry tomatoes, garlic and shallots to the skillet and place over medium heat. Mix in the lemon zest and juice and then, once the fettuccine is done, drain and add it to the skillet as well. Toss and mix well, until the pasta is completely coated.

Once the pasta is nice and coated, add the burrata. You will want to break it open and spread over the top so it really mixes in well. Pop the skillet into the oven and heat for 3 to 4 minutes, letting the burrata melt slightly. Remove from the oven and top with your vine tomatoes. Most of the ingredients in this dish are already poppin' with flavor, but our final touch will be grating your cured egg yolk on top. This is going to give your dish that umami salt pop that Parmesan cheese would, with an extra depth because, well, it's egg yolk!

*This is such an impressive and tasty dish and it comes together so easily! Garlic and shrimp are a match made in heaven, and the sauce is packed full of flavor. The crème fraîche makes it nice and creamy, transforming this already great seafood pasta into something heavenly. There's not much better than a big bowl of pasta with a sauce made of wine, butter, garlic and crème fraîche!*

# GARLIC SHRIMP LINGUINE

## Elevated with Creamy Crème Fraîche White Wine Sauce

**Prep time: 20 minutes · Cook time: 15 minutes · Servings: 4**

**Garlic Shrimp Linguine**
1 lb (455 g) shrimp
2 cloves garlic, minced
1 tbsp (15 ml) olive oil
1/2 tsp red pepper flakes
1 lb (455 g) dried linguine (see Notes)
Fresh parsley, for garnish

**Creamy White Wine Sauce**
1/3 cup (80 ml) white wine
3 tbsp (43 g) unsalted butter
3 cloves garlic, minced
1/2 cup (120 ml) vegetable stock
3 tbsp (45 ml) fresh lemon juice
1 tbsp Dijon mustard
1/2 tsp salt
1 1/2 cups (225 g) cherry tomatoes, sliced in half
1/2 cup (50 g) thinly shredded Parmesan cheese, plus more for serving
1/2 cup (115 g) crème fraîche

First things first: For the linguine, let's get the shrimp marinating! Peel and dry your shrimp, then place in a medium-sized bowl. Toss with the garlic, olive oil and red pepper flakes. Let marinate for about 20 minutes. While they marinate, bring a heavy-bottomed pot of water to a boil for the linguine, but don't add the noodles to it yet.

When the shrimp are done marinating, heat a large nonstick skillet over medium-high heat, then cook the shrimp mixture for about 3 minutes on each side. Once the shrimp are cooked, transfer to a plate and set aside.

Make the white wine sauce: Pour the white wine into the same skillet, as used for the shrimp to deglaze, scraping up all the bits of garlic that are left from the shrimp. Let the white wine cook off a bit, about 3 minutes, and then add your butter. Once the butter is melted, add your garlic and cook for another minute. Pour in the vegetable stock and lemon juice and stir in the Dijon mustard and salt. Bring to a boil and add your cherry tomatoes. Lower the heat to medium and let cook for about 10 minutes. This is when you want to add your linguine to the pot of boiling water, because it takes 10 to 12 minutes to cook.

Once the sauce has reduced a bit and become a little thicker, bring down its heat to low and add your Parmesan cheese and crème fraîche; stir until fully incorporated. By now, your noodles should be done, so drain and transfer them to the large skillet that contains the sauce. Coat the linguine with the sauce and add the shrimp back to the skillet. Serve with a sprinkle of Parmesan cheese and fresh parsley.

**Notes**

1- *You can use whatever kind of pasta you'd like; it doesn't have to be linguine.*

2- *Feel free to place the shrimp in individual bowls instead of the big skillet of noodles, if you have a picky eater.*

**PAIRINGS**

**3-Step Stuffed Pears Packed with Prosciutto, Blue Cheese and Walnuts (page 63)**

**Easy Blender Muffin Pan Popovers with Strawberry Butter (page 102)**

**PAIRINGS**

Classic Wedge Salad with Blue
Cheese Dressing and Cured Egg
Yolk (page 98)

Blood Orange Custard
Layer Cake Made Easy with
Marshmallow Meringue Frosting
(page 122)

*Pumpkin pasta is a must for the fall season, and it'll keep you cozy all through winter, too. This dish becomes a showstopper with the goat cheese and crème fraîche that make it creamy and rich, the andouille sausage that comes in with a hint of spice, and of course, don't forget the sweet, crunchy pop from the brown butter walnut sage crumble on top!*

# PUMPKIN PASTA WITH ANDOUILLE SAUSAGE

## Made Special with Crème Fraîche and Brown Butter Walnut Sage Crumble

**Prep time: 10 minutes · Cook time: 20 minutes · Servings: 4**

### Brown Butter Walnut Sage Crumble

2 tbsp (28 g) unsalted butter
7 to 8 sage leaves
1/2 cup (60 g) walnuts, chopped
2 tsp (10 g) light or dark brown sugar
1/2 tsp salt

### Pumpkin Pasta

1 lb (455 g) dried pasta (see Notes)
12 oz (340 g) andouille sausage, sliced into medallions (see Notes)
2 tbsp (28 g) unsalted butter
4 cloves garlic, minced
1 (15-oz [425-g]) can pumpkin puree
1 cup (240 ml) vegetable or chicken stock
1/2 cup (75 g) goat cheese, plus more for serving
1/2 cup (115 g) crème fraîche
1/2 tsp salt
Freshly ground black pepper (optional)

Make the crumble: In a medium-sized skillet, melt the butter over medium heat. Once it starts to foam and brown, add your sage leaves and allow them to crisp up (this should take less than 3 minutes). Transfer the leaves to a paper towel-covered plate. Add the walnuts to the pan and toast for about 5 minutes, then transfer to a small bowl. Crumble the sage leaves into the bowl (reserving a few whole crispy leaves for serving, if you wish), then add the brown sugar and salt. Mix well and set aside.

Make the pasta: In a saucepan, cook the pasta according to the package instructions. Meanwhile, in a large skillet, arrange the sausage slices in a single layer and let brown for 8 to 10 minutes. Once browned, transfer the sausage to a plate.

Allow the pan to cool slightly, then add the butter. Once it starts to brown, add your garlic. Let the garlic cook for 30 seconds, or until fragrant (be careful not to let it burn), then add the pumpkin puree. Add the stock and mix until fully incorporated. Once smooth, add the goat cheese, crème fraîche, salt and pepper to taste (if using).

Drain the pasta, return it to the saucepan used to cook it and add the andouille sausage. Mix until completely coated. Serve with a goodly amount—at least 1 tablespoon (15 ml)—of brown butter walnut sage crumble on top. I like to top it with extra goat cheese and crispy sage leaves!

### Notes

1- *You can use any kind of pasta for this recipe, but I prefer rigatoni because the ridges allow the sauce to cling to the pasta.*

2- *Just leave out the andouille sausage and use vegetable stock to have a delicious vegetarian dish.*

*We all need a one-pan dish up our sleeve, don't you think? Well, this is mine! I have been making this for so long, I figured it was time to actually write it down and share it with the world. This dish is veggie packed and uses the best noodles (in my opinion) that exist on the planet— udon! Udon know what you've been missing until you try this dish (Get it? Wink wink). Elevating this dish is the incredible sauce that uses miso paste to kick it up to an umami bomb!*

# ONE-PAN UDON NOODLE STIR-FRY

## with Oyster Sauce Made Explosive by Miso Paste

**Prep time: 15 minutes · Cook time: 20 minutes · Servings: 4**

### Stir-Fry

2 lb (905 g) frozen or dried udon noodles

3 tbsp (45 ml) sesame oil, divided

2 tbsp (30 ml) olive oil

1 shallot, sliced thinly

2 cloves garlic, minced

1 cup (91 g) small broccoli florets

1/2 red bell pepper, seeded and sliced thinly

1 1/2 cups (105 g) sliced baby bella mushrooms

Green onions, sliced thinly, for serving

Sesame seeds, for serving

### Sauce

2 tbsp (30 ml) oyster sauce

2 tbsp (30 ml) soy sauce

2 tbsp (28 g) dark brown sugar

1 tbsp (15 ml) rice vinegar

1 tsp garlic chili paste

1 tbsp (16 g) brown rice miso paste

1 tsp molasses

1 tsp grated fresh ginger

2 cloves garlic, minced

Make the stir-fry. If your udon noodles are frozen you are going to want to thaw them by heating a large pot of water until it starts to simmer, not boil. Carefully drop in the noodles and gently separate with tongs. After about 2 minutes, the noodles will separate easily; at this point, drain and place them in a large bowl. Drizzle 1 tablespoon (15 ml) of the sesame oil over them and toss. (If using dried noodles, follow the package instructions to cook them, then drain and add 1 tablespoon [15 ml] of sesame oil.) Set aside.

In a large wok or a large skillet, heat your olive oil over medium heat. Toss in your shallot and let it cook down for 3 minutes. Add your garlic, broccoli, red bell pepper and mushrooms and let them cook down for about 10 minutes.

While the stir-fry vegetables and aromatics cook, make your sauce: In a medium-sized bowl, combine the oyster sauce, soy sauce, brown sugar, rice vinegar, garlic chili paste, miso paste, molasses, ginger and garlic and stir until well combined.

Once your stir-fry mixture is cooked to perfection, transfer it from the wok to a plate and set aside. Add the remaining 2 tablespoons (30 ml) of sesame oil to the wok and heat over medium–high heat. Once the sesame oil is hot, add the udon noodles. Pour the sauce over the noodles and toss to mix. Let your noodles sit in the pan for 3 to 4 minutes to crisp up. Flip them to another side and repeat until the noodles are as crispy as you'd like, then add your stir-fry mixture back to the wok. Toss to mix well, and then serve sprinkled with your thinly sliced green onions and sesame seeds.

### Note

1- *Feel free to mix up the veggies you use for this dish. It's a great meal for the "whatever veggies are left in the fridge" day.*

## PAIRINGS

**Thai Tea Panna Cotta with Mango Lassi Crema and Peanut Cashew Crumble (page 113)**

**Easy Deviled Eggs Made Restaurant Worthy by Marinating in Soy Sauce with a Creamy Sriracha Filling (page 67)**

*Introducing the recipe from the cover of my book, ladies and gentlemen! This is also one of the recipes I am most proud of, since it started as a random idea I had and actually ended up working (after a couple of mistrials, of course). Not only that, but this pot roast is insanely flavorful. By adding red wine, soy sauce and my, well, now not-so-secret ingredient, dark chocolate, this dish is completely filled with powerful umami flavors. Topping it with homemade biscuits was the crazy idea I had that I can now say works perfectly. It's the thing you never knew you were missing about pot roast: a biscuit topping! This is one of my favorite "set-it-and-forget-it" recipes for when you want to impress but don't want a ton of hands-on time!*

# ELEVATED RED WINE AND DARK CHOCOLATE POT ROAST

## with Homemade Mini Biscuit Topping

**Prep time: 20 minutes** · **Cook time: 3 hours** · **Servings: 4**

### Pot Roast

1 tsp salt

1 tsp garlic powder

½ tsp freshly ground black pepper

3 lb (1.4 kg) chuck roast

3 tbsp (45 ml) vegetable oil

2 cups (480 ml) beef stock, divided

2 large onions, cut into large slices

6 cloves garlic: 3 minced, 3 left whole

2 cups (480 ml) dry red wine (cabernet)

½ cup (120 ml) soy sauce

1 tbsp (15 ml) Worcestershire sauce

¼ cup (33 g) finely chopped dark chocolate

3 large carrots

8 oz (226 g) small potatoes, halved or quartered

3 thyme sprigs

1 tbsp (8 g) cornstarch + 1 tbsp (15 ml) water, for a slurry

Let's get this baby cooking! First, let me assure you that even though your pot roast will cook for a long time (the time actually flies by), you only have 20 to 30 minutes max of hands-on time. This is just one of those recipes for which you have to be mindful of when you want it to be done. If you intend to eat at around 6:00 p.m. (that's generally dinnertime for us over here), I would start the pot roast no later than 2:30 p.m.

For the pot roast, preheat the oven to 300°F (150°C). Meanwhile, you are going to hard sear the roast: In a small bowl, mix together the salt, garlic powder and pepper together and then season your roast well on all sides. In a large Dutch oven, heat the vegetable oil over medium-high heat. Once the oil is shimmering, add the seasoned roast and sear for 5 to 6 minutes on each side, making a nice crust. Remove the roast from the Dutch oven and set aside.

To the same Dutch oven (no need to clean), add 1 cup (240 ml) of the beef stock and scrape the bottom to loosen all the bits from the roast. Add the onions and minced garlic and cook down for 5 minutes. Once the onions are soft, add the remaining cup of the beef stock and the red wine, followed by the soy sauce, Worcestershire sauce and dark chocolate. Stir until well combined and then add the roast back to the pot, along with the carrots, potatoes and whole garlic cloves. Nestle everything in together so as to be covered by some of the liquid, then top with the thyme sprigs. Cover and roast in the oven for 2½ to 3 hours. This is the "set it and forget it" part.

## Biscuit Topping

4 cups (500 g) all-purpose flour, plus more for dusting

2 tbsp (28 g) baking powder

2 tsp (12 g) sea salt

1/2 cup (1 stick/114 g) unsalted butter, frozen

2 cups + 1 tbsp (495 ml) buttermilk, divided

1/2 cup (50 g) thinly shredded Parmesan cheese

1 tsp fresh thyme

## PAIRINGS

**3-Step Stuffed Pears Packed with Prosciutto, Blue Cheese and Walnuts (page 63)**

**Blood Orange Custard Layer Cake Made Easy with Marshmallow Meringue Frosting (page 122)**

When the pot roast is done (everything will be *very* tender), remove from the oven and make your biscuits: In a large bowl, combine your flour, baking powder and salt and mix well. Take your butter out of the freezer and, using a cheese grater, grate it into the flour mixture. Then, using your hands, mix it into the flour mixture until the butter feels distributed and is pea-sized throughout the flour. Slowly add 2 cups (475 ml) of buttermilk while mixing and *barely* combine. Add the Parmesan cheese and thyme and mix very carefully. The dough will be very shaggy, so once it comes together slightly, dump it out onto a lightly floured work surface and gently knead until it comes together more. You will want to fold it in on itself like a book a couple of times, taking one end and folding up and over to the center, and then the other end up and over that. Once you have folded it a couple of times, flour a rolling pin and gently roll out the dough until it's about 1/2 inch (1.3 cm) thick. Flour a 2-inch (5-cm) round cookie cutter and start cutting out biscuit rounds, but *don't* twist the cookie cutter; just go straight down and back up, or they won't rise the same.

Increase the oven temperature to 500°F (260°C). Now that everything is prepared, you can transfer the pot roast and veggies (leaving the juices in the Dutch oven) to a wider, oven-safe serving dish and top with the biscuits. Brush the biscuit tops with the remaining tablespoon (15 ml) of buttermilk. Bake for 10 to 12 minutes, or until biscuit tops are browned and they look cooked through. While the biscuits cook, put the Dutch oven with the remaining juices back on the stove over medium-high heat. In a small bowl, mix your cornstarch and water together to form a slurry, then add that to the juices. Cook down until it's reduced and thicker.

Once the biscuits have risen nicely and are browned, remove the entire dish from the oven. When you have served out the pot roast individually, drizzle the gravy you made from the juices over the top.

*See photo on page 22.

**PAIRINGS**

**3-Step Stuffed Pears with Prosciutto, Blue Cheese and Walnuts (page 63)**

**Best Ever Apple Upside-Down Cake with Buttermilk and Chai Spice (page 126)**

*When you boil balsamic vinegar, it reduces to a sweet and tangy sauce that adds an intense pop of flavor to anything it touches. Well, for this recipe, we are going to straight-up marinate a pork tenderloin in it! Pairing this with a sage apple chutney was just a no-brainer, because we all know that pork and apples are a match made in heaven.*

# MARINATED PORK TENDERLOIN WITH APPLE CHUTNEY

## Made Sweet and Tangy with Balsamic Reduction

**Prep time: 1 hour • Cook time: 40 minutes • Servings: 4**

### Pork

12 oz (340 g) pork tenderloin
$1/4$ cup (60 ml) balsamic reduction (see page 15), plus more for serving
2 tbsp (30 ml) olive oil
1 tsp smoked paprika
$1/2$ tsp salt
3 cloves garlic, minced

### Sage Apple Chutney

2 tbsp (28 g) unsalted butter
$1/2$ yellow onion, small diced
2 apples, cored and small diced
6 dried apricots, chopped
1 tbsp (15 ml) balsamic reduction (see page 15)
$1/4$ cup (60 ml) pure maple syrup
$1/4$ tsp salt
$1/4$ tsp ground cinnamon
1 tbsp (15 ml) olive oil
5 large sage leaves

Let's start by marinating the pork: Get your tenderloin ready by slicing off any silver skin or fatty parts. I use a large ziplock bag for marinating; alternatively, you can use a large lidded plastic container or glass bowl. In that bag or vessel, combine the pork, balsamic reduction, olive oil, smoked paprika, salt and garlic. Make sure the tenderloin is nice and covered with the liquid. Marinate for at least 1 hour, up to overnight. The marinade is what makes this dish so special—the sweet and tangy balsamic reduction tenderizes but also infuses the pork with so much flavor, it's incredible!

Preheat the oven to 425°F (220°C). Line a small baking sheet with aluminum foil and place your tenderloin in the center. Pour all the marinade juices over the top and slightly tent the aluminum foil over the top of the tenderloin. Bake for 30 to 45 minutes, depending on the thickness of your pork. You want the internal temperature to be 145°F (63°C) before removing from the oven.

While the tenderloin bakes, make the sage apple chutney: In a small saucepan over medium heat, melt the butter. Add the onion and cook for 5 minutes. Next, add the apples, apricots, balsamic reduction, maple syrup, salt and cinnamon and cook down for another 10 to 15 minutes. Meanwhile, in a small skillet, heat your olive oil over high heat. Once the oil is shimmering, add your sage leaves and let them get super crispy. This will take only about 1 minute; immediately transfer them to a paper towel–lined plate. When the chutney is nice and tender, crumble the sage leaves into the chutney and stir to combine.

When the pork tenderloin reaches 145°F (63°C), remove it from the oven and allow it to rest for 5 minutes. Slice into medallions and serve with a drizzle of balsamic reduction and side of sage apple chutney.

*I know a lot of people think tofu is flavorless, and they aren't wrong. What they don't know, though, is that it is the perfect blank canvas! Seriously, it will take on whatever seasonings you give it, and that makes it one of the most incredible things you can cook with. This chipotle sauce is packed with umami and it's topped with a cooling crème fraîche, making this tofu one of the most flavorful things you have ever eaten!*

# EVERYDAY CHIPOTLE TOFU BURRITO BOWLS

## with Lime Crème Fraîche Crema

**Prep time: 15 minutes · Cook time: 15 minutes · Servings: 4**

### Chipotle Sauce Tofu

2 (14-oz [400-g]) blocks extra-firm tofu
1 tbsp (15 ml) soy sauce
1 tbsp (8 g) cornstarch
1/4 cup (60 ml) olive oil, divided
2 chipotles in adobo sauce
1/2 medium-sized onion
2 cloves garlic
1 tbsp (15 ml) white wine vinegar
1 tsp ground cumin
1 tsp salt
1/4 tsp chili powder
1/4 cup (60 ml) water
1 tsp fresh lime juice

### Crème Fraîche Crema

1/2 cup (115 g) crème fraîche
1 tsp fresh lime juice
1/2 tsp hot sauce

### Burrito Bowls

Cooked rice
Sautéed bell peppers
Corn
Avocado or guacamole crema
Fresh cilantro
Cotija cheese

First things first: Prepare the tofu. You will need to press your tofu for at least 15 minutes. This will help release some of the water from it. You can do this with a tofu press (we eat tofu enough that I bought one and it's amazing), or you can place the tofu on a plate and layer heavy things on top, such as a cast-iron skillet. While it is pressing, preheat the oven to 450°F (230°C) and line a large baking sheet with parchment paper.

Once your tofu is pressed, cut it into 1-inch (2.5-cm) cubes. Place the cubes in a large bowl or large ziplock bag, add the soy sauce, cornstarch and 1 tablespoon (15 ml) of the olive oil and toss until well coated. Place the coated tofu on the prepared baking sheet and bake for 15 minutes. Remove from the oven, flip all the pieces over and bake for another 10 minutes.

While the tofu bakes, make the chipotle sauce; this is where this dish really comes together. In a blender, combine the remaining 3 tablespoons (45 ml) of olive oil, chipotles (removed from the adobo sauce), onion, garlic, vinegar, cumin, salt, chili powder, water and lime juice and blend on high speed for about 1 minute, or until smooth.

Go ahead and make the crema now, too: In a small bowl, mix together the crème fraîche, lime juice and hot sauce, then set aside.

Once the tofu is done, toss the cubes into a large nonstick skillet over medium heat. Pour in the chipotle sauce, over the tofu. Cook down for about 5 minutes, or until the tofu is nice and coated and the sauce has thickened. Remove from the heat.

Assemble your bowls! Place some rice in each bowl, then add some chipotle sauce tofu, sautéed bell peppers, corn, avocado, crema, cilantro and Cotija cheese, and serve.

**PAIRINGS**

**Effortless Garlic Confit Feta Dip Packed with Herbs and Sun-Dried Tomatoes (page 75)**

**Explosive Red Wine Ganache Tart with Raspberry Jam Layer and Chocolate Crust (page 130)**

*Garlic beats pretty much everything, can we agree? Well, maybe besides garlic butter. Let's add some umami poppin' miso paste, and we are at an all-new high. Now, imagine a delicious rib eye coated in this miso garlic butter. This dish is here to make your weeknight a little bit more special, and delicious.*

# WEEKNIGHT STEAK TIPS
## with Miso Garlic Butter

**Prep time: 30 minutes · Cook time: 10 minutes · Servings: 4**

1¹/₂ lb (680 g) rib eye
Salt and freshly ground black pepper
1 tbsp (15 ml) olive or avocado oil
¹/₄ cup (57 g) unsalted butter, divided
5 cloves garlic, minced
1 tbsp (16 g) miso paste

Take the steak out of the fridge 30 minutes prior to cooking for best results. Cut into 1-inch (2.5-cm) cubes and generously coat with salt and pepper.

In a large cast-iron skillet, heat the oil over medium-high heat. When the oil is almost smoking, add 1 tablespoon (14 g) of the butter. Once it's almost completely melted, add cubes of steak in a single layer. Don't overcrowd; sear in batches, if needed. Sear them for 3 minutes on one side without moving them, then flip them over and sear for another 1 to 2 minutes, or until they reach your desired temperature; 135°F (57°C) is medium rare, which is the temperature I always try to hit. Once the bites are at your preferred temperature, transfer them to a plate. Repeat until all the rib eye is cooked.

When all the steak is out of the skillet, add the remaining 3 tablespoons (43 g) of butter to the pan. Reduce the heat to medium-low. Once it's melted, add the minced garlic and miso paste, cook for about 30 seconds to 1 minute, then remove from the heat and add the steak bites back to the skillet. Coat all the steak bites with the miso garlic butter and serve immediately.

**PAIRINGS**

**3-Step Stuffed Pears with Prosciutto, Blue Cheese and Walnuts (page 63)**

**Classic Wedge Salad with Blue Cheese Dressing and Cured Egg Yolk (page 98)**

*This meal is, by far, one of my favorites in this entire cookbook. I make it once a week; the end result is literally the most delicious chicken I've ever tasted, and I've had some tasty chicken. The marinade is crazy-packed with flavor and the chicken just soaks it all up. Miso paste and soy sauce give the chicken an umami pop, and the pickle and lemon juices make it tender beyond belief. Trust me, this recipe will become a staple in your life.*

# EVERYDAY CHICKEN SKEWERS

## with Flavor-Popping Miso Marinade

**Prep time: 30 minutes · Cook time: 15 minutes · Servings: 4**

### Marinated Chicken

3 chicken breasts, diced into 1" (2.5-cm) cubes

1/2 cup (120 ml) olive oil

1/2 cup (120 ml) soy sauce

Juice of 1/2 lemon

1 tbsp (15 ml) Dijon mustard

1 tbsp (16 g) brown rice miso paste

1/4 cup (60 ml) pickle juice, straight from the jar

1 tsp onion powder

1 tsp dried parsley

1/2 tsp salt

1/2 tsp smoked paprika

1 tbsp (15 g) light brown sugar

### Skewers

1 sweet onion, cut into quarters

1 red bell pepper, cut into 1 1/2 to 2" (4- to 6-cm) squares

1/2 pineapple, peeled, cored and cubed

Marinate your chicken: Place your cubed chicken in a large glass bowl. In a medium-sized bowl, stir together the olive oil, soy sauce, lemon juice, Dijon mustard, miso paste, pickle juice, onion powder, parsley, salt, paprika and brown sugar. Pour most of the mixture over the chicken (you want to reserve some for brushing on at the end). Marinate in the fridge for at least 30 minutes, up to 2 hours.

If using a grill, preheat your grill to 350°F (180°C). Alternatively, you can heat your oven to 425°F (220°C), but I really, really want to stress how good these are on the grill.

Assemble the kebabs: Alternate chicken, onion, bell pepper and pineapple until you fill up each skewer. Discard the marinade that the chicken had marinated in.

Place the kebabs next to one another on the grill, close but not touching. Cook for 12 to 15 minutes, depending on the size of the chicken chunks, rotating the skewers every 4 minutes. They are done when the chicken reaches 165°F (74°C). If baking, place the skewers in a single layer on a large, ungreased baking sheet. Cooking in the oven will take 15 to 20 minutes and will not get the chicken as crispy, but it will be delicious nonetheless. No need to rotate if using the oven.

Once the chicken reaches 165°F (74°C), remove from the grill and let sit for 5 minutes. Coat with the reserved marinade.

### Notes

1- *If you use bamboo skewers, be sure to soak them in water for at least 20 minutes before assembling the kebabs.*

2- *Mix up your skewer ingredients! You can use all kinds of things, including mushrooms, zucchini, peaches . . . seriously, the list is endless!*

**PAIRINGS**

Simple Loaded and Smashed
Potatoes with Hot Honey Crème
Fraîche Drizzle (page 90)

Easy Stuffed Baked Apples Made
Restaurant Worthy with Brie and a
Quick Caramel Sauce (page 117)

**PAIRINGS**

Classic Wedge Salad with Blue
Cheese Dressing and Cured Egg
Yolk (page 98)

Blood Orange Custard
Layer Cake Made Easy with
Marshmallow Meringue Frosting
(page 122)

*We don't eat a ton of meat in my house, but when we do, it's usually chicken, and most of the time we prepare it this way! This dish is so easy that it is my go-to dinner every Wednesday night. This recipe uses one of my favorite elevated ingredients that would surprise you: crème fraîche! That simple addition makes the meatballs juicier and more tender than you've ever tasted!*

# EFFORTLESS CHICKEN MEATBALL MARINARA

## Made Incredibly Juicy with Crème Fraîche

**Prep time: 10 minutes · Cook time: 30 minutes · Servings: 4**

1 (24-oz [680-g]) jar marinara sauce

### Meatballs
1 lb (455 g) ground chicken
1 large egg
½ cup (54 g) dried bread crumbs
½ cup (50 g) shredded Parmesan cheese
2 tbsp (30 g) crème fraîche
1 tsp garlic powder
½ tsp smoked paprika
1 tsp Italian seasoning
½ tsp onion powder
½ tsp salt

### Topping
1 to 2 cups (112 to 224 g) shredded mozzarella cheese

### For Serving
Cooked pasta or rice

This comes together so easily, you are not only going to be obsessed with the taste, but with the preparation (or lack thereof). First, preheat the oven to 400°F (200°C) and get out a large ovenproof pan. My go-to is my 11-inch (28-cm) cast-iron skillet. Go ahead and pour your marinara sauce into the skillet and swirl it around to evenly coat the pan. Set aside.

Make the meatballs: In a large glass bowl, mix together the ground chicken, egg, bread crumbs, Parmesan cheese, crème fraîche, garlic powder, paprika, Italian seasoning, onion powder and salt until well combined. Form 12 to 15 meatballs, depending on the size you prefer, and place them directly on top of the layer of sauce in your ovenproof pan. Bake them at 400°F (200°C) for 30 minutes, or until the meatballs reach 165°F (74°C).

Add the topping: Remove the pan from the oven and sprinkle your shredded mozzarella cheese all over the meatballs. Place back in the oven for 3 minutes, or until the cheese has melted. Let cool for 5 to 10 minutes because they will be extremely hot, then serve on top of pasta or rice.

**Notes**

1- *The leftovers from this meal make awesome chicken meatball sandwiches!*

*Honey mustard and salmon just work. The flavors are meant to go together. This delicious salmon dinner is a showstopper yet, seriously, is one of the easiest recipes in this entire cookbook. I have even made an entire fillet for dinner for two and then saved the rest to top my salads for the rest of the week. It's fancy yet feasible, and that's my favorite combination!*

# SATISFYING SALMON WITH LEMON BUTTER ORZO

### Elevated with a Flavor-Packed Honey Mustard Glaze

**Prep time: 10 minutes · Cook time: 15 minutes · Servings: 4**

### Honey Mustard Salmon

1 entire salmon fillet (about 2 lb [905 g])
1 tbsp (15 ml) whole-grain mustard
1 tbsp (15 ml) Dijon mustard
2 cloves garlic, minced
2 tbsp (30 ml) honey
1/4 tsp red pepper flakes
1/2 tsp smoked paprika
1/2 tsp salt
1 tbsp (14 g) unsalted butter, melted
1 tbsp (15 ml) fresh lemon juice
Parsley, for garnish (optional)

### Lemon Butter Orzo

1 cup (170 g) dried orzo
2 1/2 cups (600 ml) vegetable stock
1 tsp salt
1/2 tsp garlic powder
1 tbsp (14 g) unsalted butter
1 1/2 tsp (8 ml) lemon juice
2 tbsp (7 g) chopped green onion

This recipe comes together in under 30 minutes! First, we'll make the salmon: Preheat the oven to 400°F (200°C) and line a large baking sheet with parchment paper. I like to cook this as a whole fillet, but you can also portion it out, which you will want to do first if going that route. Place your salmon on the prepared baking sheet. In a small bowl, stir together the whole-grain and Dijon mustards, garlic, honey, red pepper flakes, paprika, salt, melted butter and lemon juice. Brush the mixture heavily onto your salmon, then cook for 8 to 10 minutes, or until the salmon is 125°F (52°C).

While the salmon cooks, make the lemon butter orzo: In a medium-sized saucepan, combine the orzo, vegetable stock, salt and garlic powder. Bring to a boil, then reduce the heat and simmer for 15 minutes, or until most of the liquid is absorbed. Turn off the heat and add the butter, lemon juice and green onion. Mix until fully incorporated, then serve immediately with the salmon. Garnish with parsley, if using.

### PAIRINGS

**Brussels Sprouts Salad with Roasted Red Pepper Aioli and Parmesan Crisps (page 94)**

**Explosive Red Wine Ganache Tart with Raspberry Jam Layer and Chocolate Crust (page 130)**

*Salmon doesn't have to be boring. This dish makes the most delicious and flavor-banging salmon I've ever had. The sauce is packed with big umami flavors and searing it on the stove makes it nice and crispy. The Sriracha mayo sauce adds a spicy yet cooling aspect to the whole dish, and all the additional sides keep your taste buds on their toes!*

# EASY MISO SALMON BITE BOWL

## with Creamy Sriracha Sauce

**Prep time: 10 minutes · Marinating time: 30 minutes · Cook time: 15 minutes · Servings: 4**

### Salmon

3 tbsp (45 ml) soy sauce
1 tbsp (16 g) brown rice miso paste
1 tbsp (15 ml) rice vinegar
1 tsp grated fresh ginger
2 cloves garlic, minced
1 tsp Sriracha
1 tbsp (15 ml) pure maple syrup
2 tbsp (30 ml) water
2 tbsp (30 ml) olive or avocado oil, divided
1 lb (455 g) center-cut salmon, cut into 1" (2.5-cm) pieces

### Sauce

½ cup (120 ml) mayonnaise (homemade is best!)
1 tbsp (15 ml) Sriracha
1 tsp rice vinegar

### Bowl

Seasoned cooked white or brown rice
Sliced avocado
Edamame
Sautéed baby bella or shiitake mushrooms
Kimchi
Microgreens

First, let's get your salmon marinating: In a small bowl, stir together the soy sauce, miso paste, rice vinegar, ginger, garlic, Sriracha, maple syrup, water and 1 tablespoon (15 ml) of the oil until well combined. Place the salmon in a large bag or bowl, add the marinade and let soak, refrigerated, for 30 minutes, up to 2 hours. You don't want to marinate the fish longer than 2 hours because it will start to break down, so I really recommend 30 minutes.

While the salmon marinates, you can prepare mostly everything else, since salmon doesn't take long to cook. Make the sauce: In a small bowl, stir together the mayonnaise, Sriracha and rice vinegar.

To cook the salmon, heat a large cast-iron or heavy-bottomed skillet over medium-high heat, and add the remaining tablespoon (15 ml) of oil. When the oil is shimmering, add just the salmon pieces, leaving the marinade in the bag or bowl for now. Cook for 2 to 3 minutes per side. Remove from the heat, then add the marinade to the pan and let it get nice and thick. This will end up turning into a crazy, flavorful sauce that will completely coat the salmon bites!

Assemble your bowls: Create a layer of rice, then add your salmon bites, avocado, edamame, mushrooms, kimchi and microgreens in a circular pattern around the rice.

### PAIRINGS

Thai Tea Panna Cotta with Mango Lassi Crema and Peanut Cashew Crumble (page 113)

Easy Deviled Eggs Made Restaurant Worthy by Marinating in Soy Sauce with a Creamy Sriracha Filling (page 67)

*This recipe is a staple in my weekly rotation of meals because not only does it taste amazing, but this sauce is virtually going to blow your mind. When you combine Dijon mustard, soy sauce and maple syrup, you get an incredible depth of flavor. Each of these ingredients is packed with umami, so when you combine the sweet and saltiness of them, it is pure magic. You could eat this dish every single day and not get sick of it (okay, well, maybe not every day, but you get the idea). You don't need a special occasion to have an umami bomb dinner!*

# QUICK AND EASY UMÃMI TOFU BOWL

## Made Restaurant Worthy with Sticky Dijon Soy Maple Sauce

**Prep time: 15 minutes • Cook time: 30 minutes • Servings: 4**

### Tofu

2 (14-oz [400-g]) blocks extra-firm tofu

3 tbsp (45 ml) soy sauce, divided

1 tbsp (15 ml) olive oil

1 tbsp (8 g) cornstarch

2 tbsp (30 ml) Dijon mustard

3 cloves garlic, minced

1 tbsp (15 ml) water

1 tbsp (15 ml) pure maple syrup

1 tsp Sriracha, or more (see Notes)

### Bowl

Cooked white or brown rice

Edamame

Sautéed mushrooms

Kimchi

Sliced avocado

Microgreens

Sesame seeds

Prepare your tofu: You will need to press it for at least 15 minutes, up to an hour. You can do this with a tofu press (we eat tofu enough that I bought one and it's amazing) or you can place the tofu on a plate and layer heavy things on top, such as a cast-iron skillet. Preheat the oven to 450°F (230°C) and line a large baking sheet with parchment paper.

Once your tofu is pressed, cut it into 1-inch (2.5-cm) cubes. Place in a large bowl or large ziplock bag, add 1 tablespoon (15 ml) of the soy sauce plus the olive oil and cornstarch and toss until well coated. This will give the tofu a nice crispy outside before we coat it in our sticky umami sauce. Place the coated tofu on the prepared baking sheet and bake for 15 minutes. Remove from the oven, flip all the pieces over and bake for another 10 minutes.

When the tofu is in the oven, make your sauce: In a small bowl, stir together the remaining 2 tablespoons (30 ml) of soy sauce, Dijon mustard, minced garlic, water, maple syrup and Sriracha until well combined. Once the tofu comes out of the oven, place it in a medium-sized skillet over medium heat. Pour in the sauce and allow it to coat the tofu. Cook until thickened all over, about 5 minutes.

Assemble your bowls: First, place the rice in the center, then portion out the tofu, edamame, sautéed mushrooms, kimchi, avocado and microgreens. Sprinkle with sesame seeds.

### Notes

1- *Feel free to add whatever you want to your bowls. I included what I generally eat with it, but the options are endless.*

2- *The amount of Sriracha in the sauce is not really enough to make it spicy. You can add more if you want to spice this dish up!*

## PAIRINGS

**Thai Tea Panna Cotta with Mango Lassi Crema and Peanut Cashew Crumble (page 113)**

**Easy Deviled Eggs Made Restaurant Worthy by Marinating in Soy Sauce with a Creamy Sriracha Filling (page 67)**

*You'll be putting the bang bang back in your belly with these bowls! The shrimp is crispy with not only a bangin' sweet and spicy sauce but a bangin' mango salsa to match. It's the perfect recipe to spice up your weekday meals.*

# BANG BANG SHRIMP BOWLS

## with Flavor-Popping Spicy Mango Salsa

**Prep time: 10 minutes** · **Cook time: 6 minutes** · **Servings: 4**

### Mango Salsa

1 mango, peeled, pitted and small diced

$1/2$ cucumber, small diced

$1/2$ red onion, small diced

$1/2$ jalapeño, seeded for less spice (can keep the seeds for more spice) and small diced

Juice of $1/2$ lime

Pinch of salt

### Shrimp

1 tbsp (15 ml) olive oil

$1/2$ cup (60 g) all-purpose flour

$1/2$ tsp garlic powder

$1/2$ tsp onion powder

$1/2$ tsp salt

1 lb (455 ml) shrimp, shelled and dried

$1/2$ cup (120 ml) mayonnaise (homemade is the best!)

1 tbsp (15 ml) pure maple syrup

1 tsp Sriracha

$1/2$ tsp rice vinegar

### For Serving

Seasoned cooked rice

Avocado

Green onions

Sesame seeds

First, let's make the salsa that pumps up this entire recipe. In a medium-sized bowl, combine the mango, cucumber, red onion, jalapeño, lime juice and salt, letting them marinate together while you make everything else. The combination of jalapeño and mango make these bowls sweet *and* spicy.

Next, we want the shrimp to be nice and crispy. So, in a large nonstick skillet over medium-high heat, heat the olive oil until it shimmers. In a medium-sized bowl, mix together the flour, garlic powder, onion powder and salt, and then, working in batches, toss in the shrimp, making sure to coat on all sides. Cook the shrimp in the skillet for 3 minutes per side or until crispy. Transfer to a paper towel-lined plate to let some of the excess oil soak up.

Now, we need to put the bang bang in this dish! Make the sauce while the shrimp are cooling slightly: In a large bowl, combine the mayonnaise, maple syrup, Sriracha and rice vinegar. Coat the shrimp completely by tossing them into the bowl of sauce.

Serve with rice, avocado, green onions, sesame seeds and a big scoop of your mango salsa.

### Notes

1- *This bang bang sauce is delicious with crispy fried tofu, too!*

### PAIRINGS

**Easy Deviled Eggs Made Restaurant Worthy by Marinating in Soy Sauce with a Creamy Sriracha Filling (page 67)**

**Thai Tea Panna Cotta with Mango Lassi Crema and Peanut Cashew Crumble (page 113)**

*These tacos are unlike any others you have ever had. Not only are they packed with powerful umami flavors, but they also have a sweet and tangy thing going for them with the delicious mango crema. Add some crunchy quick-pickled cabbage and you are in for a wild Taco Tuesday!*

# THE BEST EVER UMAMI SHRIMP TACOS

### with Quick Pickled Cabbage and Lime Mango Crema

**Prep time: 2 hours and 30 minutes • Cook time: 6 minutes • Servings: 4**

### Quick Pickled Cabbage

1/4 head red cabbage, shaved thinly (about 1 cup [90 g])
3/4 cup (180 ml) water
3/4 cup (180 ml) apple cider vinegar
1 tsp salt
1 tsp sugar

### Shrimp

1 tbsp (15 ml) Dijon mustard
3 tbsp (45 ml) soy sauce
1 tbsp (16 g) miso paste
1 tbsp (15 ml) water
1 lb (455 g) shrimp, peeled

### Mango Crema

1 mango, peeled, pitted and cubed
1 tbsp (15 ml) fresh lime juice
2 tbsp (2 g) finely chopped fresh cilantro
1/2 cup (120 ml) plain yogurt

### For Assembly

Corn or flour street taco-style tortillas (see Notes)
Sliced avocado
Cotija cheese
Fresh cilantro

First things first: Let's start the quick pickled cabbage so it can spend as long as possible pickling before we make these delicious tacos! Place your shaved cabbage in a glass jar; I used a 1-pint (475-ml) Mason jar. In a small saucepan, bring the water, vinegar, salt and sugar to a boil, then remove from the heat and pour over the cabbage. It's best to let the cabbage pickle for about 2 hours before serving, and it only gets better with time.

Now, let's get those shrimp into the most umami-packed shrimp marinade you've ever tasted! In a medium-sized bowl or ziplock bag, combine the Dijon mustard, soy sauce, miso paste and water, and mix until well combined. Add the shrimp and let marinate for about 30 minutes.

While the shrimp marinates, make the mango crema: This tasty crema gives a nice, cooling aspect to tacos, along with a sweetness and tanginess that you probably haven't had in a taco before. All you have to do is, in a blender, combine the mango, lime juice, cilantro and yogurt and blend until smooth and creamy.

After the shrimp has marinated for about 30 minutes, it's time to cook it: In a large nonstick skillet over medium-high heat, cook the shrimp for about 3 minutes on each side. Transfer to a plate and get prepared to assemble some of the best tacos you've ever eaten. I start by warming some street taco-style tortillas in the oven. Then, you want to layer the quick pickled cabbage on the bottom, top that with your flavor-packed shrimp and drizzle with the sweet and tangy mango crema. Add some avocado slices, Cotija cheese and more cilantro to taste, and you will be in umami heaven!

### Notes

1- *To heat the street taco tortillas, preheat the oven for 350°F (180°C), wrap your tortillas in aluminum foil and heat for 6 to 8 minutes.*

## PAIRINGS

**Easy Deviled Eggs Made Restaurant Worthy by Marinating in Soy Sauce with a Creamy Sriracha Filling (page 67)**

**Thai Tea Panna Cotta with Mango Lassi Crema and Peanut Cashew Crumble (page 113)**

*Looking for an easy summer dinner? Look no further. This galette is here for you when you want to use up all those beautiful tomatoes you have from your garden (or farmers' market or, hey, just the grocery store—no judgment). It takes minimal effort, and barely any hands-on time. If you can slice a tomato, you got this. This recipe uses two of my favorite elevated ingredients: roasted garlic and balsamic reduction! Hopefully, by now you always have balsamic reduction in your fridge, but if not, that's also a breeze to make. It's just an all-around easy, breezy and beautiful summer dinner.*

# EASY ROASTED GARLIC TOMATO GALETTE

## Made Sweet and Tangy with Balsamic Reduction

**Prep time: 15 minutes · Cook time: 35 minutes · Servings: 4**

Balsamic Reduction
(see page 15)

*Galette*

3 large tomatoes, sliced thinly
1 (9" [23-cm]) premade piecrust
3 heads garlic, roasted
(see page 13)
Salt, for finishing
1/4 cup (25 g) finely shredded
Parmesan cheese
Fresh thyme, for garnish

First, preheat the oven to 400°F (200°C) and line a large baking sheet with parchment paper. Next, make the balsamic reduction. You can find an in-depth how-to on page 15.

While it reduces, assemble your galette: Lay out your tomato slices on a clean kitchen towel or paper towels to drain some of the liquid. Flip them once and let dry out until you need them.

Unroll your premade pie dough (another great part about this recipe) and spread your roasted garlic in the center, leaving a 1-inch (2.5-cm) bare border. Layer your tomatoes in a circular pattern, starting from the outside and working your way in. Using the outside border you left on your piecrust, fold the dough slightly over the tomatoes and ruffle it, keeping the center exposed. Bake for 35 minutes, or until the dough is nice and browned.

Remove from the oven and sprinkle with salt, Parmesan cheese and fresh thyme. Drizzle some balsamic reduction over the top and serve warm.

## PAIRINGS

Classic Wedge Salad with Blue Cheese Dressing and Cured Egg Yolk (page 98)

Blood Orange Custard Layer Cake Made Easy with Quick Marshmallow Meringue Frosting (page 122)

*This soup is perfect for soup season and, yes, I know I say that about all the soups in my cookbook, but seriously y'all, what's better than a loaded baked potato soup? Not much, but I'll tell you why this one is the best: Coconut milk makes this soup ultra smooth and creamy but not heavy, and the crème fraîche adds depth to the creaminess. Smoky Cheddar adds a whole new flavor to the average potato soup, and of course, crispy pancetta is the cherry on top, bringing all the salty goodness. You won't want to go back to your basic potato soup after making this one; that's a guarantee!*

# LOADED POTATO AND LEEK SOUP

## Elevated with Smoky Cheddar, Crispy Pancetta and Crème Fraîche

**Prep Time: 10 minutes** · **Cook Time: 30 minutes** · **Servings: 4**

4 oz (115 g) pancetta, chopped, or 6 slices bacon

2 leeks, white bottom part only, sliced thinly

1 head garlic, roasted (see page 13)

3 tbsp (43 g) unsalted butter

1/4 cup (30 g) all-purpose flour

3 cups (720 ml) vegetable stock

2 lb (905 g) golden potatoes, cut into small cubes

1/2 tsp salt

1/4 tsp freshly ground black pepper

1 cup (240 ml) coconut milk

1/2 cup (115 g) crème fraîche (see Notes)

1 cup (113 g) shredded smoky Cheddar cheese, plus more for garnish

3 to 4 green onions, sliced, for garnish

In a large Dutch oven or heavy-bottomed pot, cook your pancetta over medium-high heat until crispy. Transfer to a paper towel-lined plate and set aside to use for topping. Lower the heat to medium and add your leeks. Sweat them for about 5 minutes, or until they become slightly translucent, then add the garlic and let cook for another minute.

Add the butter, and once it's melted, whisk in the flour and cook for 1 minute, or until golden. Whisk in the vegetable stock, then add the cubed potatoes. Partially cover, allowing for some steam to escape and let cook for 15 to 20 minutes over medium-low heat.

Using an immersion blender, blend the potato mixture together in the pot until almost completely smooth; I like to leave a little bit of chunks for texture. Once it's blended and smooth, stir in your salt, pepper, coconut milk, crème fraîche and Cheddar cheese. Cook for another 5 to 10 minutes, or until the cheese is melted and everything is completely combined. Serve in soup bowls, topped with the crispy pancetta, green onions and a sprinkle more of Cheddar cheese.

### Notes

1- *I prefer using an immersion blender for this; they are inexpensive and amazing to have on hand. If using a regular blender, you will need to work in batches and return the blended mixture to the pot. An immersion blender allows you to blend everything at once, and you can leave it as chunky as you'd like!*

2- *You can also substitute sour cream for the crème fraîche, but I highly suggest using the crème fraîche, if you can!*

**PAIRINGS**

**Classic Wedge Salad with Blue Cheese Dressing and Cured Egg Yolk (page 98)**

**Simple Apple Hand Pies Stuffed with Brown Butter Apples and Chunks of Brie (page 107)**

*This fall soup season is going to be unlike any other once you experience this recipe. Roasted poblanos elevate this dish by adding a subtle spice and charred flavor that makes this the soup you didn't know you were missing until now. The spicy poblanos mixed with sweet corn and coconut milk end up making a flavor-packed sweet and spicy soup that will have your taste buds firing on all cylinders.*

# SWEET CORN SOUP

## Made Extraordinary with Roasted Poblanos and Cotija Cheese

**Prep time: 45 minutes** · **Cook time: 25 minutes** · **Servings: 4**

5 poblano peppers
2 tbsp (28 g) unsalted butter
2 shallots, thinly sliced
3 cloves garlic, minced
2 tbsp (15 g) all-purpose flour
3½ cups (840 ml) vegetable stock
3 cups (462 g) corn (from around 6 ears)
1 tsp salt
1 cup (240 ml) coconut milk
1 tbsp (15 ml) fresh lime juice
Fresh cilantro, for serving
Cojita cheese, for serving
Pepitas or pumpkin seeds, for serving

Let's elevate this dish right off the bat by roasting the poblanos! Preheat the oven to 400°F (200°C). Line a baking sheet with aluminum foil and place all the poblanos in a single layer on the prepared pan. Roast for 45 minutes. They won't need any oil or seasoning because we are just trying to char the outside and make the inside more flavorful.

Once your poblanos are nice and charred, cut off the stems and either leave in all the seeds for a stronger heat, remove half of them for a medium heat or remove them all for a milder heat. I like to keep half and remove half because I like a milder spice level but, if you want to turn up the heat, leave all those bad boys in and go for it!

In a large Dutch oven or heavy-bottomed pot, melt the butter over medium-high heat and add the shallots. Cook those down for a couple of minutes, then add the garlic and cook for another 30 seconds. Whisk in the flour to make a sort of roux and cook until it is golden brown. Next, add your vegetable stock and bring to a simmer over medium-low heat. Cook for about 2 minutes before adding your corn, poblanos and salt. Cover and simmer for 20 minutes.

When done simmering, use an immersion blender or regular blender (you will have to do this in batches) to blend all the corn and poblanos until smooth. Lastly, stir in your coconut milk to make it ultra Add spacecreamy, and the lime juice for some tang. Serve warm, topped with cilantro, a goodly amount of Cotija cheese, plus pepitas.

## PAIRINGS

**Quick and Easy Roasted Cauliflower with Creamy Tahini Dressing and Crispy Honey Miso Chickpeas (page 97)**

**Simple Apple Hand Pies Stuffed with Brown Butter Apples and Chunks of Brie (page 107)**

### Notes

1- *If you want to remove the seeds from the poblanos, all you have to do is chop off the top after they have been roasted; generally, they pull right out from the inside.*

2- *Don't scrimp on the Cotija! It cuts the heat with a salty and cool flavor that is absolutely divine.*

# MEMORABLE STARTERS IN A SNAP

The appetizer is a very important part of a dinner. It sets the whole mood of the meal. In this chapter, you will find explosive flavor combinations packed into small packages. There are perfect party foods, such as the Flavor-Popping Stuffed Mushrooms with Caramelized Onions , Gruyère and Prosciutto (page 72), Quick Crispy Buffalo Chicken Egg Rolls with a Cooling Dill Ranch Dip (page 68) or Effortless Garlic Confit Feta Dip Packed with Herbs and Sun-Dried Tomatoes (page 75), all so flavorful and unique that your guests will never forget them. There are even recipes you can have when you just want a snack, such as the Tastiest Sourdough Bruschetta Elevated with Flavorful Herb Oil and Topped with Crispy Capers (page 71). All the recipes in this chapter are going to leave your taste buds dancing and ready for more!

*POV: You're hosting a party and you have a million things to do. Take a load off your plate by putting these pears on them! Nothing screams "elevated party food" like prosciutto, blue cheese, walnuts and Bosc pears. This is such an impressive dish, and here's a little secret: It's probably the easiest one in this entire cookbook! Simply made, with complex flavors. Monumental taste, with little to no hands-on time. That, right there, is the way I like to do things.*

# 3-STEP STUFFED PEARS

## Packed with Prosciutto, Blue Cheese and Walnuts

**Prep time: 10 minutes** • **Cook time: 30 minutes** • **Servings: 10 pear halves**

5 Bosc or Bartlett pears

1 tsp fresh lemon juice

1/3 cup (45 g) crumbled blue cheese

1/3 cup (40 g) chopped walnuts

1/3 cup (50 g) chopped prosciutto

1 tbsp (14 g) unsalted butter, melted

1 tbsp (15 ml) cider vinegar

1 tbsp (13 g) granulated sugar

1/2 tsp salt

1/4 tsp freshly ground black pepper

Let's get started by preheating the oven to 375°F (190°C). Prep the pears by slicing them in half lengthwise and scooping out the core and seeds. Place the pears in a large ovenproof dish, such as an 11-inch (28-cm) cast-iron skillet. I like to slice a little piece off the center of the back of each pear half so it will sit sturdily. Sprinkle them all with your teaspoon of lemon juice to keep them from browning.

In a medium-sized bowl, mix together your flavor-popping filling, a.k.a. the blue cheese, walnuts and prosciutto, until well incorporated. In a small bowl, mix together the butter, vinegar, sugar, salt and pepper. Brush this mixture all over the pears, and then place about 1 tablespoon (15 ml) of the blue cheese mixture in the center of each pear (where you scooped out the core). Stuff the filling down a bit to ensure the pears are full.

Bake for 30 minutes, or until everything is nice and melty and the pears have slightly browned. These come out *beautiful*. Seriously, a showstopper. Serve immediately; they are definitely best warm right out of the oven!

### PAIRINGS

**Simple Summer Fettuccine Made Restaurant Worthy with Cherry Tomato Garlic Confit Sauce (page 25)**

**Approachable Mini Cinnamon Pavlovas Elevated with Brown Butter Caramelized Apples (page 111)**

### Notes

1- *You can make these ahead and then bake right before you need them. Just follow all steps until baking, cover with plastic wrap and keep in the fridge. When you're ready to cook, just preheat the oven to 375°F (190°C) and bake for 30 minutes.*

*Get ready for soup season with this belly- and soul-warming roasted butternut squash, apple and onion soup topped with spicy andouille sausage. Coconut cream and Cheddar cheese make this already flavor-packed soup ultra creamy and delicious. Roasting the fruits and veggies with cinnamon adds a warmth and depth, and adding ginger and curry powder provides a nice, low-key spiciness that pairs perfectly with the sweet squash apple and onion combo. Top with salty andouille sausage and we have now hit every single flavor profile imaginable!*

# APPROACHABLE AUTUMN SQUASH SOUP

## with Andouille Sausage, Cheddar and Coconut Milk

**Prep time: 45 minutes • Cook time: 20 minutes • Servings: 6**

1 butternut squash (about 2 lb [905 g])

2 apples

2 onions

3 tbsp (45 ml) olive oil

1 tsp ground cinnamon

1/2 tsp cayenne pepper

4 andouille sausages, small diced

3 large sage leaves, chopped

3 cloves garlic, minced

1 tsp ground ginger

2 tsp (4 g) curry powder

3 cups (720 ml) vegetable stock

1 (15-oz [425-g]) can coconut cream

1/2 tsp salt

1 cup (113 g) shredded Cheddar cheese

Preheat the oven to 400°F (200°C) and line a large baking sheet with aluminum foil. Peel and dice the butternut squash, apples and onions. Toss with the olive oil, sprinkle with the cinnamon and cayenne pepper, then spread on the prepared baking sheet. Bake for 45 minutes, or until tender.

While the fruits and veggies bake, heat a large Dutch oven or heavy-bottomed pot over medium-high heat. Cook the andouille sausages in the pot until crispy, 8 to 10 minutes, adding the sage leaves halfway through the cooking time to crisp up. Transfer the sausage mixture to a paper towel-lined plate and set aside.

We really kick up the flavor with this next part. Place the garlic into the Dutch oven, along with the ginger and (my favorite secret ingredient) curry powder, and cook for 30 seconds. The veggies should be done baking by this time, so add them to the pot. Pour in the vegetable stock and coconut cream, add the salt and simmer, covered, over low heat for 15 minutes.

When the 15 minutes are up, using an immersion blender (or a stand blender, working in batches), blend everything until it's nice and smooth. Lastly, add the cheese and stir until melted and well incorporated. The soup should be crazy smooth and creamy by now. Serve in a soup bowl with the andouille sausage and extra crispy sage leaves on top and enjoy the warm feeling in your heart and belly!

**Notes**

1- *This soup could easily become a main course if you wanted to serve it in a larger portion for those who love a hearty, belly-filling soup for dinner.*

**PAIRINGS**

**Easy Roasted Garlic Tomato Galette Made Sweet and Tangy with Balsamic Reduction (page 55)**

**Epic Small-Batch Chocolate Chip Cookies Made Bakery Worthy with Miso Brown Butter (page 108)**

*You've never seen deviled eggs this way; trust me! If we are being honest, they are just a crazy idea I had that actually ended up being really tasty. If you get anything from this recipe, besides how incredibly delicious it is, you should get that sometimes you just need to go for it! I thought, Hey, maybe I can twist a classic so far that it just may work, and it did! The flavors in this dish are exciting and enticing and will have your taste buds dancing like no one's watching.*

# EASY DEVILED EGGS

## Made Restaurant Worthy by Marinating in Soy Sauce with a Creamy Sriracha Filling

**Prep time: 15 minutes** • **Cook time: 10 minutes** • **Marinating time: 6 hours** • **Servings: 12 deviled eggs**

### Marinated Eggs

1 cup (240 ml) water
1 tbsp (15 g) dark brown sugar
1/2 cup (120 ml) soy sauce
1/4 cup (60 ml) rice vinegar
1 clove garlic, smashed
1/4 tsp red pepper flakes
2 green onions, sliced thinly
6 hard-boiled large eggs, peeled

### Filling

6 hard-boiled egg yolks
3 tbsp (45 ml) mayonnaise (homemade is the best!)
1 tbsp (15 ml) Sriracha
1 tsp rice vinegar
2 tsp (10 ml) Dijon mustard

### Optional Garnishes

Sesame seeds
Green onions

First, we will marinate the eggs: In a small saucepan, combine the water, brown sugar, soy sauce, rice vinegar, garlic, red pepper flakes and green onion, bring to a boil, then simmer over medium-low heat for 3 minutes. Place your hard-boiled eggs in a tight-fitting, lidded jar (I used a pint-sized [475-ml] Mason jar), and pour the marinade over them. Once cooled to room temperature, cover and place in the fridge for 6 hours, or up to overnight.

Make the filling: Once the eggs have soaked, slice them in half and pop out the yolks into a medium-sized bowl. Set the whites aside. Mix the mayonnaise, Sriracha, rice vinegar and Dijon mustard into the egg yolks until smooth. Fill the inside cavity of each egg white with the filling and garnish, if desired, with sesame seeds and green onions.

### PAIRINGS

**Quick and Easy Umami Tofu Bowl Made Restaurant Worthy with Sticky Dijon Soy Maple Sauce (page 48)**

**Epic Small-Batch Chocolate Chip Cookies Made Bakery Worthy with Miso Brown Butter (page 108)**

*When you think of egg rolls, I bet you think mainly Asian flavors, right? Well, that wouldn't be very exciting of me to put in a cookbook filled with recipes that have fun and exciting elevated flavor twists, now would it? These crispy, crunchy rolls are filled with a perfectly spicy and cool Buffalo chicken and blue cheese mixture that is going to make your taste buds sing!*

# QUICK CRISPY BUFFALO CHICKEN EGG ROLLS

### with a Cooling Dill Ranch Dip

**Prep time: 10 minutes • Cook time: 10 to 12 minutes • Servings: 10**

### Dill Ranch Dip

1/3 cup (80 ml) mayonnaise (homemade is the best!)
1/3 cup (80 ml) sour cream
1/3 cup (80 ml) buttermilk
3 tbsp (10 g) finely chopped fresh dill
1 tsp fresh lemon juice
1 tsp Worcestershire sauce
1/2 tsp garlic powder
1/4 tsp salt
1/4 tsp onion powder

### Buffalo Chicken Egg Rolls

2 cups (280 g) shredded cooked chicken
4 oz (115 g) cream cheese, at room temperature
1/2 cup (68 g) crumbled blue cheese
1/2 cup (58 g) shredded Cheddar cheese
2 celery ribs, chopped
1/4 cup (60 ml) Buffalo sauce
1 (1-lb [455-g]) package egg roll wrappers
Olive or avocado oil, for brushing

First, make the ranch because the flavor gets better with time. In a medium-sized bowl, combine the mayonnaise, sour cream, buttermilk, dill, lemon juice, Worcestershire sauce, garlic powder, salt and onion powder and mix well. Keep in the fridge until needed.

For the egg rolls, in a large bowl, combine the shredded chicken, cream cheese, blue cheese, Cheddar cheese, celery and Buffalo sauce and mix until well incorporated.

Set out a small bowl of water. Lay out an egg roll wrapper in a diamond shape with one of the points nearest you. Place about 1 tablespoon (15 ml) of filling right above that corner. Dip your finger in the water and run it along the entire edge of the wrapper. Now, starting at the point closest to you, pull that end of the wrapper up and over the filling, tucking it in a tiny bit underneath the filling. Next, pull the right-side point over to the center and then repeat with the left-side point. Once both sides are folded in toward the middle, you will roll the filling forward until the rest of the wrapper has been tucked in underneath it. Repeat with the rest of the wrappers and filling.

Preheat an air fryer to 380°F (193°C). Working in batches, brush the egg rolls with a small amount of oil and then place in the air fryer, not letting them touch one another. Cook for 10 to 12 minutes, or until golden brown. Repeat until they are all done.

### Notes

1- *If you overfill the centers of your egg rolls, they will burst in the air fryer.*

2- *Alternatively, bake in a preheated 400°F (200°C) oven for 10 to 12 minutes. To cook on the stovetop, fill a large, deep skillet with about 2 inches (5 cm) of oil and heat over medium heat. Add a couple of egg rolls at a time and fry, flipping them over after a couple of minutes, until golden brown. Drain on paper towels.*

**PAIRINGS**

Easy Roasted Garlic Tomato
Galette Made Sweet and Tangy
with Balsamic Reduction (page 55)

Best Ever Apple Upside-Down
Cake with Buttermilk and Chai
Spice (page 126)

PAIRING

Blood Orange Custard Layer
Cake Made Easy with Box
Cake and Quick Marshmallow
Meringue Frosting (page 122)

*This is quite a twist on the average bruschetta. Crispy sourdough bread and juicy roasted tomatoes alone can make your taste buds very happy, but top that with some crispy capers and a basil-infused olive oil, and you have a work of art in food form.*

# TASTIEST SOURDOUGH BRUSCHETTA

## Elevated with Flavorful Herb Oil and Topped with Crispy Capers

Prep time: 10 minutes · Cook time: 25 minutes · Servings: 6

### Herb Oil
2 cups (80 g) fresh basil
³/₄ cup (175 ml) high-quality olive oil

### Roasted Tomatoes
4 cups (600 g) cherry tomatoes
2 tbsp (30 ml) olive oil
1 tsp salt
¹/₂ tsp freshly ground black pepper

### Sourdough
1 (2-lb [905-g]) loaf sourdough bread (or French bread or another white bread of your choice)
2 tbsp (30 ml) olive oil
Flaky sea salt

### Crispy Capers
2 tbsp (17 g) capers
¹/₄ cup (60 ml) olive oil

Preheat the oven to 400°F (200°C). First, you will want to make your herb oil. This may sound intimidating, but it is easy-peasy lemon squeezy! Bring a small pot of water to a boil and prepare an ice bath (bowl of ice and water). Blanch your basil by putting it into the boiling water for 20 seconds and then transfer it directly into the ice bath; let cool for 5 minutes. Remove from the ice bath, lay your basil in a clean tea towel or paper towels, then try to wring out as much water as possible. Now, in a blender, combine the basil and oil and blend until smooth. Strain through a fine-mesh sieve, removing all the basil pulp. What you have left is a bright green basil-infused olive oil!

Next, roast the tomatoes: On a large baking sheet, combine the tomatoes, olive oil, salt and pepper and mix well so the tomatoes are completely coated. Roast in the oven for 20 to 25 minutes, or until they have slightly burst. Remove from the oven and let cool.

Once the tomatoes come out of the oven, get your sourdough ready. Slice at least six slices of sourdough, place on a second baking sheet, then drizzle both sides with the olive oil and sprinkle with flaky sea salt. Toast in the oven for 5 to 8 minutes, just giving a light toast.

While the bread toasts, make the crispy capers: First, drain the capers and dry them as best you can by spreading them on a paper towel-lined plate. In a small saucepan over medium heat, heat your olive oil. Once the oil is shimmering, add your capers and let them crisp up for 3 to 5 minutes. You will be able to tell when they start to get crispy by their outer shells getting flaky. Once they are crispy enough for you, transfer them to a separate paper towel-lined plate to let drain.

Now, it's time to assemble your bruschetta! Lay down the sourdough slices, then layer your burst cherry tomatoes on top. Sprinkle some crispy capers over the tomatoes, then drizzle with your herb oil.

### PAIRING
Weeknight Steak Tips with Miso Garlic Butter (page 39)

*The perfect party food doesn't exist . . . wait a minute. These stuffed mushrooms are the perfect party food! Easy to make, packed full of flavor and enough to go around? Yes, please! Buttery and tender caramelized onions pair perfectly with rich Gruyère cheese and salty prosciutto to create a tasty combination that will surprise everyone. They may seem little but they explode with flavor in your mouth and will quickly become a party favorite!*

# FLAVOR-POPPING STUFFED MUSHROOMS

## with Caramelized Onions, Gruyère and Prosciutto

**Prep Time: 10 minutes • Cook Time: 25 minutes • Servings: 8**

24 baby bella mushrooms
1 tbsp (14 g) butter, melted
4 oz (115 g) prosciutto, diced
2 tbsp (28 g) butter
½ large yellow onion, sliced thinly
6 oz (170 g) cream cheese, at room temperature
2 cloves garlic, minced
½ cup (58 g) shredded Gruyère cheese
½ tsp salt
Dried parsley (optional)

Preheat the oven to 400°F (200°C). Line a large baking sheet with parchment paper. Carefully clean all your mushrooms with a damp towel or lightly rinse under running water. Remove the stems and save them for later (not needed in this recipe, but great for a stir-fry). Brush the top of each mushroom with the melted butter and place them, top side down, on the prepared baking sheet.

Now, let's start making the flavor-poppin' mixture to stuff inside our mushrooms: In a large sauté pan over medium heat, crisp up your prosciutto for about 5 minutes. Transfer to a paper towel-lined plate. Lower the heat to medium-low and add the 2 tablespoons (28 g) of butter and the onion. Caramelize the onion for about 10 minutes, or until soft and browned. Remove the mixture from the heat.

In a large bowl, mix together the cream cheese, garlic, Gruyère cheese, prosciutto, caramelized onions and salt until well combined. Stuff about 1 to 2 teaspoons (5 to 10 ml) of filling into each mushroom cap. You want to slightly overstuff and then push down the filling to make sure they are filled all the way. Bake for 20 to 25 minutes, or until the cheese is melted and bubbly. Garnish with dried parsley, if using.

**PAIRINGS**

**Simple Summer Fettuccine Made Restaurant Worthy with Cherry Tomato Garlic Confit Sauce (page 25)**

**Best Ever Apple Upside-Down Cake with Buttermilk and Chai Spice (page 126)**

*This is the perfect party dip if you have no time for a bunch of extra steps. There is pretty much one step in this entire recipe, and the outcome is an insanely flavorful dip that anyone you serve it to will love. Tangy feta, sweet roasted garlic, juicy tomatoes and enough herbs to make your heart sing.*

# EFFORTLESS GARLIC CONFIT FETA DIP

## Packed with Herbs and Sun-Dried Tomatoes

Prep time: 5 minutes • Cook time: 40 minutes • Servings: 8

1 (8-oz [225-g]) block feta cheese
5 to 6 cherry tomatoes, sliced in half
1 small shallot, sliced
1/3 cup (18 g) sun-dried tomatoes
1 head garlic, peeled and broken apart into cloves
1/3 cup (20 g) fresh dill, chopped finely
2 tbsp (8 g) finely chopped fresh parsley
Salt and freshly ground black pepper
1 1/2 to 2 cups (360 to 480 ml) avocado or olive oil

"Flavor poppin" gets a whole new meaning when it comes to this dip. Let's start by preheating the oven to 400°F (200°C). Place the block of feta in a small ovenproof baking dish and surround with the halved cherry tomatoes, shallot, sun-dried tomatoes and garlic cloves. Sprinkle the dill, parsley, salt and pepper on top and then pour the oil over all until it covers everything.

Bake for 35 to 40 minutes, or until bubbly and the garlic is tender. Serve with crusty bread or chips.

### Notes

*1- You can use this for a pasta sauce base, too! Follow the instructions for my Simple Summer Fettuccine with Cherry Tomato Garlic Confit Sauce (page 25) and just substitute this recipe for the tomato confit recipe.*

## PAIRINGS

Everyday Chicken Skewers with Flavor-Popping Miso Marinade (page 40)

Blood Orange Custard Layer Cake Made Easy with Box Cake and Quick Marshmallow Meringue Frosting (page 122)

*These fries are going to be your new favorite comfort food! You're not going to be able to stop eating them, and I'm not going to apologize for that because you will be so happy the whole time. Think of these steak fries as fancy fair food: doused in smoky Cheddar cheese and crème fraîche sauce, topped with an entire rib eye steak cooked to perfection (well, that part's on you, but I believe in you).*

# NEXT LEVEL CHEESE STEAK FRIES

## with Smoky Cheddar Crème Fraîche Cheese Sauce

**Prep time: 20 minutes • Cook time: 20 minutes • Servings: 4**

### Steak Fries
12 oz (340 g) rib eye
1 tsp salt
2 lb (905 g) frozen french fries
2 tbsp (30 ml) canola or vegetable oil
2 tbsp (28 g) unsalted butter
2 cloves garlic, peeled and smashed

### Cheese Sauce
1 tbsp (14 g) butter
1 tbsp (8 g) all-purpose flour
1/2 cup (120 ml) whole milk
2 tsp (12 g) salt
1/4 tsp garlic powder
1 1/2 cups (170 g) shredded smoky Cheddar cheese
1/2 cup (115 g) crème fraîche
Fresh parsley, for garnish

The way I prep my steak for cooking is by heavily salting it and leaving it to dry in the fridge for at least 30 minutes (can be refrigerated for hours, if you want to get started on it early). About 30 minutes before you are getting ready to prepare this dish, remove your steak from the fridge to let it come to room temperature. Soak up any excess liquid with a paper towel, sprinkle each side with salt and press in. Set aside.

Cook the fries according to their package instructions. You can also totally make fries from scratch, but they can be super tricky, so I like to take the shortcut and use frozen fries!

While the fries cook, let's cook the steak. Once the steak has come to room temperature, heat a cast-iron skillet over medium-high heat for a couple of minutes. Then heat your oil (we use canola oil so it doesn't burn as fast). Once it's shimmering, add your steak and let it sear for 3 minutes without moving it. Then, flip it, add the butter and your garlic cloves to the pan, then let sear for another 3 minutes. Flip again and, using a spoon, baste the steak in butter for 1 to 2 minutes, then flip one last time and baste again. You're aiming for 125 to 130°F (52 to 54°C), medium rare. Once the steak is done, let it rest on a plate for 15 minutes before slicing.

**PAIRINGS**

**Weeknight Steak Tips
with Miso Garlic Butter
(page 39)**

**Best Ever Apple Upside-
Down Cake with
Buttermilk and Chai
Spice (page 126)**

While the steak rests, let's make the flavor-packed cheese sauce: In a small saucepan over medium heat, melt the butter. Once it has melted, whisk in the flour and let cook for about 1 minute, or until golden and bubbly. Next, add a small amount of milk at a time, whisking constantly. The mix will start to get clumpy, then smooth out. Once all the milk is added and the mixture is smooth, add the salt and garlic powder. Then, handful by handful, add your cheese and let it melt down. Cook until everything is smooth and melted. I like to run my sauce through a fine-mesh sieve to get out any of the cheese wax that comes with most smoky Cheddars. Remove from the heat, strain if you'd like and pour into a bowl. Lastly, add your crème fraîche and stir until completely incorporated.

Now, all we need to do is assemble: Arrange a bed of fries on a large serving dish. Thinly slice the ribeye and cut it into small bite-sized pieces. Sprinkle the steak all over the top of the fries, then drizzle the whole thing with your sauce, garnish with parsley and enjoy!

*These crispy grit cakes are topped with a sweet cherry tomato garlic confit and drizzled with the most flavorful olive oil you will ever taste. Make these for your next party and your guests are going to be blown away. For sure, they have never had anything like this before, because I'm pretty certain I made it up!*

# SOUTHERN COMFORT GOUDA GRIT CAKES

## Topped with Cherry Tomato Garlic Confit

Prep time: 15 minutes • Cook time: 1 hour • Cool time: 4 hours to overnight • Servings: 8

### Grit Cakes

3 cups (720 ml) water
³/₄ tsp salt
1 cup (90 g) uncooked white corn grits
¹/₂ cup (58 g) shredded Gouda cheese
3 tbsp (43 g) unsalted butter, divided

### Cherry Tomato Garlic Confit

1 cup (150 g) cherry tomatoes
1 shallot, peeled and sliced thinly
¹/₂ cup (68 g) cloves garlic, peeled and left whole
1 cup (240 ml) olive oil
¹/₂ tsp salt
¹/₄ tsp freshly ground black pepper
2 sprigs rosemary
2 sprigs thyme

### Garnishes

Flaky sea salt
Microgreens

First, make your grits: Line a 7 x 11-inch (18 x 28-cm) baking dish with plastic wrap. In a medium-sized saucepan, bring the water to a boil. Once boiling, stir in your salt, then add the grits, stirring the entire time. Cook for 6 to 7 minutes, or until most of the water is absorbed. Remove from the heat and add your Gouda cheese and 2 tablespoons (28 g) of your butter. Stir until everything is melted and combined, then pour the grits into your prepared dish. Cover the top with plastic wrap and chill in the refrigerator for at least 4 hours, or overnight.

About an hour before you are about ready to eat this delicious dish, make your confit. Follow the instructions for confit on page 21, adding the tomatoes and shallot. Make sure to choose a baking dish that will fit everything.

Once that the confit is made, remove your grits from the fridge. You can cut them into whatever shape you'd like, but I made mine into little rectangles about 2 inches (5 cm) wide and 3 to 4 inches (7.5 to 10 cm) long. Once you have cut your grits into little cakes, you are going to fry them up! In a large nonstick skillet over medium-high heat, melt your last tablespoon (14 g) of butter. Once it's melted and slightly starting to brown, add your grit cakes. You will probably need to do this in two batches. Fry the cakes until browned on both sides, 3 to 4 minutes per side. Repeat until all the cakes are nice and browned.

Now, we are ready to assemble: Place the grit cakes on a plate, then top with about 2 tablespoons (30 ml) of the cherry tomato garlic confit, getting a nice mixture of tomatoes, shallots and garlic. Sprinkle each with a little flaky sea salt and top with microgreens!

**Notes**

1- *Try topping these grifts with some shrimp and a Cajun cream sauce for a little shrimp and grits action!*

## PAIRINGS

**Satisfying Salmon with Lemon Butter Orzo Elevated with a Flavor-Packed Honey Mustard Glaze (page 44)**

**Easiest Ever Blue Cheese Pear Galette with Brown Butter Walnut Sage Crumble (page 133)**

*Not only is this a recipe for gazpacho, a delicious vegetable-packed cold soup, but it also comes with a bonus recipe for marinated feta, which will quickly become one of your favorite things ever. This dish is already crazy flavorful on its own, but add some marinated feta, crispy garlic bread crumbs and a quick tomato cucumber topping, and you basically have the ultimate summer starter!*

# SIMPLE CHERRY TOMATO GAZPACHO

## Made Restaurant Worthy with Flavor-Packed Marinated Feta

**Prep time: 10 minutes** · **Cook time: 10 minutes** · **Marinating time: overnight** · **Servings: 10 pear halves**

### Marinated Feta

1 (8-oz [225-g]) block feta cheese, cut into 1" (2.5-cm) cubes

1¹/₂ cups (360 ml) olive oil

1 tbsp (4 g) chopped fresh dill

1 tbsp (4 g) chopped fresh parsley

1 tbsp (3 g) chopped fresh chives

1 tsp red pepper flakes

### Bread Crumb Topping

1 tbsp (14 g) unsalted butter

1 clove garlic, minced

¹/₂ cup (30 g) panko bread crumbs

1 tsp lemon zest

1 tbsp (4 g) chopped fresh parsley

### Gazpacho

2 lb (905 g) cherry tomatoes, divided

1 English cucumber, halved, divided

1 head garlic, roasted (see page 13)

1 shallot

¹/₄ cup (60 ml) olive oil

2 tbsp (30 ml) rice vinegar

1 red bell pepper

2 tbsp (8 g) chopped fresh dill

2 tbsp (8 g) chopped fresh parsley

First, let's marinate your life-changing feta. You will want to have this sit overnight, so do this at least 1 day ahead so it really gets to soak up the flavors. Combine the feta cheese, olive oil, dill, parsley, chives and red pepper flakes in a glass container and leave in the fridge until ready to use.

Make the bread crumb topping: In a small skillet, melt the butter. Add the garlic and cook for 30 seconds, then add the bread crumbs and lemon zest. Stir until browned, remove from the heat, then add the parsley. This is going to add a nice texture to your dish.

Finally, let's make gazpacho! It's easier than you'd think—all we need to do is, in a blender, combine 1¹/₂ pounds (680 g) of the tomatoes, half of the English cucumber, roasted garlic, shallot, olive oil, rice vinegar, red bell pepper, dill and parsley and blend until smooth. Dice the remaining ¹/₂ pound (225 g) of tomatoes and remaining half of the cucumber for topping.

Once the gazpacho is prepared, assemble the dish by pouring some gazpacho into a soup bowl and topping with four or five feta cubes, some of the diced tomato and cucumber, plus a nice sprinkle of the bread crumb topping. Drizzle some of the olive oil from the marinated feta over the top. Serve cold!

### PAIRINGS

**Garlic Shrimp Linguine Elevated with Creamy Crème Fraîche White Wine Sauce (page 26)**

**Explosive Red Wine Ganache Tart with Raspberry Jam Layer and Chocolate Cookie Crust (page 130)**

# SIMPLY STANDOUT SIDES

Every meal needs a standout side dish. Sometimes, the side dish can even be more interesting and delicious than the main course. In this chapter, there will be some sides you won't be able to stop thinking about and will want to keep making over and over with all kinds of different dinners. From Quick Full-Flavor Cheesy Grits Elevated with Roasted Garlic (page 93) to Easy Fondant Potatoes Elevated with Miso Maple Walnut Glaze (page 85) to Classic Wedge Salad with Blue Cheese Dressing and Cured Egg Yolk (page 98), there is something for everyone. This entire cookbook focuses on full-flavored foods, and I didn't scrimp on the sides. Every single one of these dishes is bold in its own way, without stealing the show (well, most of the time). There's nothing worse than a boring side dish that seems like an afterthought, and I can personally guarantee none of these will ever make you feel like that.

*This, by far, has become my favorite way to eat sweet potatoes. The potatoes themselves are crispy on the outside and crazy tender on the inside, but what really elevates this dish is its glaze. Miso paste gives the glaze a depth of saltiness and the maple adds a sweetness to balance it out. Walnuts provide the perfect crunch and the sauce just complements the potatoes more beautifully than you could ever imagine. This side dish would go perfectly with so many dishes, I can't even list them. Even better, this impressive side doesn't take much effort at all!*

# EASY FONDANT SWEET POTATOES

## Elevated with Miso Maple Walnut Glaze

**Prep time: 10 minutes · Cook time: 30 minutes · Servings: 4**

### Sweet Potatoes

2 tbsp (30 ml) olive oil

3 to 4 sweet potatoes, peeled and cut into rounds 1¹/₂" (4-cm) thick (see Notes)

¹/₂ tsp salt

¹/₄ cup (57 g) unsalted butter, divided into 4 equal-sized pieces

1 cup (240 ml) chicken or vegetable stock

Flaky sea salt, for finishing

Fresh thyme, for garnish

### Miso Maple Walnut Glaze

1 cup (117 g) walnuts, chopped small (see Notes)

2 tbsp (28 g) unsalted butter

¹/₄ cup (60 ml) pure maple syrup

1 tsp brown rice miso paste

1 tbsp (15 ml) water

First, cook the potatoes: The tenderness of these potatoes is what makes them so special. To achieve that, we need to sear and then bake them, so get the oven preheating to 400°F (200°C). Meanwhile, in a large cast-iron or any large ovenproof skillet, heat the olive oil until it shimmers. Add the sweet potato rounds evenly around the skillet and allow to sear for 5 minutes. Flip the potatoes, season evenly with the ¹/₂ teaspoon of salt and cook for another 3 minutes. Add the butter, allow to melt and foam, then pour the stock in the pan. Place in the oven and bake for 30 minutes.

While the potatoes bake, let's make the real flavor star of this dish, the glaze! In a small skillet, dry toast the walnuts for 2 to 3 minutes over medium heat, until they start to brown and you can smell the nuttiness coming off of them. Now, add your butter and mix into the walnuts. Lower the heat to low and add your maple syrup, miso paste and water. Mix well and cook down for a couple of minutes, or until thick.

Once the potatoes are done, you can either leave them in the skillet to serve or transfer to a plate. Drizzle the glaze over them, then sprinkle with some flaky sea salt and thyme. Serve warm.

### Notes

1- *When purchasing sweet potatoes for this recipe, try to find thinner ones that are about the same circumference or the entire length of the potato.*

2- *You can replace the walnuts with pecans, if you prefer.*

*I'm from the South and, if there is one thing that we know how to make there, it's biscuits. All kinds of biscuits. My personal favorite is buttermilk drop biscuits, because not only are they easy, but you can add whatever flavors you want to them. Another personal favorite of mine is Red Lobster's Cheddar Bay Biscuits®. Anyone else? Yeah, they are pretty addictive, so I decided to make my own version with, you guessed it, my favorite ingredient: roasted garlic! If you need help with roasting your garlic, visit page 13 and I'll teach you exactly how to make it! That's the precious ingredient that takes these biscuits to the next level.*

# EVERYDAY BUTTERMILK DROP BISCUITS

## with Cheddar and Roasted Garlic

**Prep time: 10 minutes • Cook time: 12 minutes • Servings: 8 to 10 biscuits**

### Biscuits

2 cups (250 g) self-rising flour

1/2 cup (114 g) unsalted butter, frozen

1 1/4 cups (280 ml) buttermilk

1 cup (113 g) shredded sharp Cheddar cheese

3 heads garlic, roasted (page 13)

1 tbsp (2 g) fresh thyme

1/4 tsp salt

Flaky sea salt, for sprinkling

### Herby Garlic Butter Topping

1/4 cup (57 g) unsalted butter, melted

1 tsp Italian seasoning

1 tsp garlic powder

1/4 tsp salt

First, make the biscuits: Preheat the oven to 450°F (230°C) and line a large baking sheet with parchment paper. Place your flour in a large bowl and then, using a cheese grater, grate your frozen butter into the flour. Mix with your hands until the butter is fully incorporated and it feels pea-sized in the flour.

Slowly add the buttermilk in a stream to your flour mixture and stir gently to incorporate. Gently fold in the Cheddar cheese, roasted garlic, thyme and salt. *Do not overmix.*

Pinch off 2 1/2 to 3 inches (6.5 to 7.5 cm) of the dough and roll roughly into a ball. You should get eight to ten balls, depending on the size. Place about 2 inches (5 cm) apart from one another on the baking sheet and sprinkle with flaky sea salt (because everything is better with a sprinkle of salt). Bake for 13 to 20 minutes, depending on the size, or until lightly browned.

While the biscuits bake, make the topping: In a small bowl, mix together the melted butter, Italian seasoning, garlic powder and salt.

Once the biscuits are done, remove them from the oven and brush your seasoned butter over the top of each. Let cool on the baking sheet for a couple of minutes and then enjoy them warm.

### PAIRINGS

**Weeknight Steak Tips with Miso Garlic Butter (page 39)**

**Blood Orange Custard Layer Cake Made Easy with Box Cake and Quick Marshmallow Meringue Frosting (page 122)**

*Everyone who has tasted this mac and cheese has been obsessed with it. Honestly, just thinking about it right now makes me want to go and make some. It combines the comfort of a creamy, classic mac and cheese with some really powerful flavors, including crème fraîche, Gruyère and white Cheddar cheese. All of that cheesiness lies just beneath a crispy, crunchy top layer made up of panko bread crumbs and a nice, thick baked layer of the two cheeses. Now, if you will excuse me, I'm going to go make myself some of this irresistible (seriously) mac and cheese because my mouth is literally watering.*

# BOUGIE BAKED MAC AND CHEESE

Made Next Level with Gruyère and Crème Fraîche

**Prep time: 15 minutes · Cook time: 25 minutes · Servings: 6**

1 lb (455 g) dried macaroni (see Notes)

1¼ cups (288 g) crème fraîche

2 cups (225 g) shredded Gruyère cheese

2 cups (225 g) shredded white Cheddar cheese

½ tsp salt

½ tsp freshly ground black pepper

½ tsp garlic powder

⅓ cup (20 g) panko bread crumbs

First things first, let's cook that pasta! Preheat the oven to 350°F (180°C). Cook your macaroni according to the package directions. Once the macaroni are done, place them in a 3-quart (2.8-L) baking dish. Mix in the crème fraîche, half of your Gruyère and white Cheddar cheeses, salt, pepper and garlic powder until fully combined.

Top the macaroni with the rest of your Gruyère and white Cheddar cheese, and then sprinkle the panko bread crumbs on top. Bake for 20 to 25 minutes, or until the bread crumbs are lightly browned.

### Notes

1- *You don't have to use elbow macaroni. In the photo here, I used cavatappi.*

2- *To make ahead, prepare the noodles and their toppings all the way through until the point of baking, cover, then store in the fridge for up to a day before baking.*

### PAIRINGS

**Marinated Pork Tenderloin with Apple Chutney Made Sweet and Tangy with Balsamic Reduction (page 35)**

**Simple Apple Hand Pies Stuffed with Brown Butter Apples and Chunks of Brie (page 107)**

*This is my reimagined baked potato recipe. I love baked potatoes; I mean, who doesn't, really? Potatoes, in general, are a glorious part of the food world and this is just another recipe to prove that. In this recipe, I go ahead and deconstruct the baked potato to make it easier to eat and serve. Then, I top it with a cooling yet slightly sweet and spicy crème fraîche drizzle to make all the rest of the flavors pop. Plus, it's always fun to smash things, am I right?!*

# SIMPLE LOADED AND SMASHED POTATOES

### with Hot Honey Crème Fraîche Drizzle

**Prep time: 5 minutes · Cook time: 20–25 minutes · Servings: 8**

2 lb (905 g) golden or Yukon Gold potatoes (about 8 small)

¼ cup (57 g) unsalted butter, melted

1 tsp salt

1½ cups (170 g) shredded Cheddar cheese

½ cup (115 g) crème fraîche

2 tsp (10 ml) hot honey

6 slices bacon, cooked and crumbled, for serving

¼ cup (12 g) finely chopped fresh chives, for serving

## Notes

*1- Get crazy with this recipe by adding all your favorite fixin's to it. You can add such things as raw or sautéed onions, green onions, sautéed peppers, jalapeños, smoky Cheddar cheese, prosciutto or pancetta instead of bacon, or whatever your favorite things are to put on baked potatoes!*

The potatoes you are going to want to use for this should be about the size of a tennis ball (maybe even a little smaller). You want them to be a substantial enough size that they will be filling, but small enough that you can actually smash one without it breaking into a million pieces. I find that a number of the Yukon Gold potatoes in a 5-pound (2.3-kg) bag work perfectly. You will want to start by washing about eight of them and then putting them in a large pot. Cover them with water and place over high heat. Sprinkle 1 to 2 teaspoons (6 to 12 g) of salt into the water and bring to a boil. Once boiling, cover the pot and lower the heat to a simmer. Let simmer for 10 to 15 minutes, or until tender and easily pierced by a fork.

While the potatoes boil, preheat the oven to 400°F (200°C) and line a large baking sheet with aluminum foil. Once the potatoes are done and tender, drain and place them about 2 inches (5 cm) apart on the prepared baking sheet. Using the bottom of a sturdy glass cup, smash each potato down enough that they break apart but still stay together. You don't want it to break into too many separate pieces, although it's not the end of the world if a few small pieces break off. Just nestle the potato piles together as best as you can.

Once all the potatoes are smashed on the baking sheet, brush the top of each with your melted butter, then sprinkle each with some of the salt. Next, you want to cover each potato with a good amount of the Cheddar cheese. Place the potatoes in the oven and bake for 5 to 8 minutes, or until the cheese is nice and melted.

While the potatoes are in the oven, in a small bowl, stir together your crème fraîche and hot honey until smooth and well mixed. As soon as the potatoes come out of the oven, sprinkle them with the bacon, chives and a drizzle of the crème fraîche mixture. Serve warm.

*Grits are kind of like the rice of the South: the blank canvas to which you can add almost any flavor and they still work. Well, this recipe takes some of my all-time favorite flavors and mixes them into a creamy and hearty dish of some of the cheesiest, most delicious grits you will ever taste. Another roasted garlic recipe? Yep! This stuff is too good to not put in anything I can, and grits are the perfect accompaniment for roasted garlic—and Gouda!*

# QUICK FULL-FLAVOR CHEESY GRITS

## Elevated with Roasted Garlic

**Prep time: 20 minutes · Cook time: 40 minutes · Servings: 6**

6 cups (1.4 L) water or vegetable stock

1 tsp salt, plus more to taste

1½ cups (135 g) uncooked stone-ground grits

3 tbsp (43 g) unsalted butter

1½ cups (170 g) shredded Gouda cheese, plus more for garnish

½ cup (58 g) shredded white Cheddar cheese, plus more for garnish

2 tbsp (30 ml) heavy cream

1 head garlic, roasted (see page 13)

Green onions, for garnish

Pepper, for garnish

In a medium-sized saucepan, bring your water and the salt to a boil. Once boiling, lower the heat to low and gently whisk in your grits, making sure they don't sink and stick to the bottom. They will start to absorb water pretty quickly, so make sure to stir every couple of minutes, scraping the bottom to keep everything moving and cooking until they reach your desired consistency. This can take anywhere from 30 (thinner grits) to 45 minutes (not-going-anywhere super thick grits).

Once they have reached your desired consistency (I like them thicker), whisk in your butter and then remove from the heat. Now, let's kick it up a notch by adding your Gouda and Cheddar cheese, cream and roasted garlic. Mix until well combined and then salt to taste. Garnish with cheese slices, green onions and pepper and serve warm.

### Notes

1- *You can use all different varieties of cheese. Mix it up and use some Gruyère instead of Gouda, or go with only Cheddar and it will be extra cheesy.*

## PAIRINGS

**Weeknight Steak Tips with Miso Garlic Butter (page 39)**

**Simple Apple Hand Pies Stuffed with Brown Butter Apples and Chunks of Brie (page 107)**

*Don't let the name fool you; this is a crazy-easy recipe to make. The aioli is going to quickly become one of your favorite dressings (or even a dip) and it can go with all kinds of things! Add some crispy Parmesan cheese chips and cured egg yolks, and this salad is a flavor bomb ready to go with your favorite dinner!*

# BRUSSELS SPROUTS SALAD

## with Roasted Red Pepper Aioli and Parmesan Crisps

**Prep time: 10 minutes** · **Cook time: 20 minutes** · **Servings: 4**

### Aioli Dressing

2 red bell peppers

1 cup (240 ml) avocado oil

1 large egg

1/4 cup (25 g) finely grated Parmesan cheese

1/2 tsp salt

2 tsp (10 ml) Dijon mustard

3 tbsp (45 ml) fresh lemon juice

1/4 tsp freshly ground black pepper

1/2 cup (115 g) crème fraîche

### Salad

1/2 cup (50 g) shredded Parmesan cheese

12 oz (340 g) Brussels sprouts

1 cup (150 g) cherry tomatoes, sliced in half

1 cured egg yolk (see page 16; optional)

For the aioli dressing, you need to roast your peppers, which are going to give this aioli dressing its big flavor twist! Preheat the oven to 450°F (230°C). Cut your red bell peppers in half lengthwise and lay, cut side down, on a foil-covered baking sheet. Roast in the oven for 15 to 20 minutes, or until charred on the outside. Remove from the oven. Once slightly cooled, gently peel off the skin. You should have about 1/4 cup (45 g) of roasted red peppers at the end of this.

In a blender, combine the roasted red bell peppers, avocado oil, egg, Parmesan cheese, salt, Dijon mustard, lemon juice, black pepper and crème fraîche. Blend for 30 seconds to a minute, or until everything is nice and smooth. Transfer the dressing to a lidded glass container and keep in the fridge until needed. Making this in advance will also help it become even more flavorful. Don't forget that you can also use this as a dip later.

Before assembling the salad, make the Parmesan crisps: Decrease the oven temperature to 350°F (180°C) and line a large baking sheet with parchment paper. On the prepared baking sheet, lay out little piles, about 2 inches (5 cm) wide and about 1/2 inch (1.3 cm) high, of the Parmesan cheese, placing them 3 inches (7.5 cm) apart. Bake for 3 minutes, or until they have melted down and browned. Remove from the oven and let cool while you make the rest of the salad. Carefully, using a mandoline (or a knife, if you don't have a mandoline), thinly shave the Brussels sprouts. Toss in a large bowl with the sliced tomatoes and some of the aioli until lightly covered. If using, grate the cured egg yolk over the top (our final elevated flourish) and garnish with the Parmesan crisps!

**PAIRINGS**

**Marinated Pork Tenderloin with
Apple Chutney Made Sweet and
Tangy with Balsamic Reduction
(page 35)**

**Best Ever Apple Upside-Down
Cake with Buttermilk and Chai
Spice (page 126)**

### PAIRINGS

Loaded Potato and Leek Soup Elevated with Smoky Cheddar, Crispy Pancetta and Crème Fraîche (page 56)

Easy Stuffed Baked Apples Made Restaurant Worthy with Brie and a Quick Caramel Sauce (page 117)

*This side dish could easily steal the spotlight at any dinner. It could also easily be turned into the main dish for a vegetarian meal. Roasted cauliflower makes a flavorful and filling base, while the lemon tahini dressing gives a lovely creamy tanginess. Oh, and we can't forget the crunch factor from the crispy honey miso chickpeas, which you are going to want to start making just to snack on, after this!*

# QUICK AND EASY ROASTED CAULIFLOWER

## with Creamy Tahini Dressing and Crispy Honey Miso Chickpeas

**Prep time: 15 minutes · Cook time: 20 minutes · Servings: 4**

### Honey Miso Chickpeas

1 (15-oz [425-g]) can chickpeas, rinsed and dried, with the skins off (see Notes)
4 tsp (20 ml) olive oil, divided
1 tsp salt
1 tbsp (15 ml) honey
1/4 tsp brown rice miso paste
1/4 tsp Sriracha

### Cauliflower

2 heads cauliflower (about 4 lb [1.8 g] total), cut into florets
2 tbsp (30 ml) olive oil
1 tsp garlic powder
1 tsp onion powder
1/2 tsp smoked paprika
1 tsp salt

### Tahini Dressing

1/3 cup (80 g) tahini
2 tbsp (30 ml) fresh lemon juice
1 tbsp (15 ml) Dijon mustard
1 tbsp (15 ml) pure maple syrup
Pinch of salt
1 clove garlic, minced
3 tbsp (45 ml) water, if needed

First, make the chickpeas: Preheat the oven to 400°F (200°C) and line a large baking sheet with parchment paper. Toss the chickpeas in 1 tablespoon (15 ml) of your olive oil and your salt, then roast them in the oven for 20 minutes. While they roast, in a medium-size bowl, stir together the remaining teaspoon of olive oil, honey, miso paste and Sriracha. When the 20 minutes are up, remove the chickpeas from the oven, add them to the honey mixture, then toss, making sure to coat them well. Pour the chickpeas back onto their baking sheet and roast for another 7 minutes, or until they are nice and crispy. Transfer to a bowl and keep nearby until the final step.

Now for the cauliflower: Leave the oven at 400°F (200°C) and discard the parchment paper from the chickpeas so you can just reuse that baking sheet, bare, for your cauliflower. Place your florets on the baking sheet, drizzle with the olive oil and sprinkle with the garlic powder, onion powder, paprika and salt. Toss and massage the florets around your baking sheet to coat the cauliflower well. Bake for 15 to 18 minutes, or until the florets are tender and slightly browned.

While the cauliflower bakes, make your tahini dressing: In a blender, combine the tahini, lemon juice, Dijon mustard, maple syrup, a pinch of salt and garlic and blend until smooth. If you need to add water, you can, little by little, until the dressing is to your desired consistency.

Once the cauliflower comes out of the oven, arrange the florets in a single layer on a large serving dish, then add a nice drizzle of the tahini dressing and top off with your flavor-packed crispy honey miso chickpeas.

**Notes**

1- *An easy way to get the chickpea skins off is by putting some between two paper towels and rolling around on the counter.*

*This is pretty much a classic that I kept classic. Sometimes, food is so delicious that you don't need to change much aside from adding one thing to really make that dish pop. That's why I decided to add my favorite special ingredient: cured egg yolk! This one ingredient can elevate this classic salad all on its own.*

# CLASSIC WEDGE SALAD

## with Blue Cheese Dressing and Cured Egg Yolk

**Prep time: 5 minutes** • **Cook time: 10 minutes** • **Servings: 4**

### Blue Cheese Dressing

1 cup (240 ml) mayonnaise (homemade is best!)

1 cup (135 g) crumbled blue cheese

3 tbsp (45 ml) buttermilk

1/2 tsp Worcestershire sauce

1 1/2 tsp (8 ml) fresh lemon juice

1/4 tsp cayenne pepper

### Wedge Salad

1 head iceberg lettuce, sliced into 4 wedges

6 slices bacon, cooked and crumbled

1 cup (150 g) cherry tomatoes

1/2 cup (68 g) crumbled blue cheese

1 cured egg yolk (see page 16)

First, let's make the dressing: In a small bowl, combine the mayonnaise, blue cheese, buttermilk, Worcestershire sauce, lemon juice and cayenne and mix really well until completely incorporated. Store in an airtight container in the fridge until needed. Making the dressing ahead of time will give the flavors longer time to meld, too.

Assemble the salad by placing a lettuce wedge on a plate and covering with the blue cheese dressing. Putting the dressing on first helps everything else stick to the wedge. Sprinkle with the bacon crumbles, cherry tomatoes and blue cheese crumbles. Now, let's elevate this dish by grating your cured egg yolk all over the top.

### PAIRINGS

Simple Summer Fettuccine Made Restaurant Worthy with Cherry Tomato Garlic Confit Sauce (page 25)

Simple Apple Hand Pies Stuffed with Brown Butter and Chunks of Brie (page 107)

*I love any vegetable I can hasselback. This is such a genius way of cooking starchy veggies—I wish I could say I came up with it! Alas, I did not, but this popular trend had me thinking about what else I could hasselback, and I thought up the perfect thing! Honeynut squash is, by far, one of my favorite squashes. It's basically a mini, sweeter butternut squash. When you hasselback it, it becomes insanely tender. Adding the miso honey butter just sends it over the edge of greatness.*

# DELICIOUS HASSELBACK HONEYNUT SQUASH

## with a Sweet and Salty Miso Honey Butter

**Prep time: 15 minutes · Cook time: 40 minutes · Servings: 4**

2 honeynut squashes
1 tbsp (15 ml) olive oil
1 tsp salt
1/2 tsp freshly ground black pepper
1/4 cup (57 g) unsalted butter, melted
1 1/2 tsp (8 g) miso paste
2 tbsp (30 ml) honey
Fresh thyme, for garnish

### PAIRINGS

Simple Summer Fettuccine Made Restaurant Worthy with Cherry Tomato Garlic Confit Sauce (page 25)

Epic Small-Batch Chocolate Chip Cookies Made Bakery Worthy with Miso Brown Butter (page 108)

First things first: Preheat the oven to 400°F (200°C). Carefully peel the skin off the honeynut squashes, using a vegetable peeler and then, even more carefully, slice each squash in half lengthwise. Scrape or scoop out the stringy insides and seeds. Now, lay one squash half cut side down, and place two wooden spoon handles, or chopsticks if you have them, along each side of it. Using a knife, slice crosswise into the squash every 1/2 inch (1.3 cm), all the way down the length of the squash, stopping each time where your knife hits the wooden spoon handles. This creates the hasselback effect! Repeat with the rest of the squash halves, then place them all in a large baking dish, brush with your olive oil and sprinkle with the salt and pepper. Bake for 20 minutes.

While they bake, mix up the miso honey butter: This sauce is *divine* and can be added to all kinds of vegetables, so definitely keep it in your back pocket. All you have to do is, in a small bowl, whisk together the melted butter, miso paste and honey until well combined. Now, once the first 20 minutes of baking time is up, pull the squash out of the oven and brush with some of the miso honey butter. Put it back in the oven to bake for 10 more minutes.

The key to this recipe is to baste the squash multiple times with the miso honey butter, so it really soaks it up. Once the 10-minute baking time is up, remove from the oven and brush again with miso honey butter. Bake one more time for 10 minutes, then remove from the oven, brush one last time with miso honey butter and sprinkle with fresh thyme leaves. Serve warm.

*I've always loved popovers, but they are a little daunting to make. You need a special pan, there are a lot of steps and a lot of things that can go wrong. Well, not with this recipe! You almost can't mess these up because, truthfully, they aren't really popovers. They are like a mix between a German pancake, mini Dutch baby and a popover. They make an amazing dinner roll and get even better with homemade strawberry honey butter.*

# EASY BLENDER MUFFIN PAN POPOVERS

## with Strawberry Butter

**Prep time: 10 minutes** · **Cook time: 18 minutes** · **Servings: 12 popovers**

### Popovers

Nonstick olive oil spray

6 large eggs

1 cup (125 g) all-purpose flour

1 cup (240 ml) milk

1/4 cup (57 g) unsalted butter

1/2 tsp salt

1/2 tsp vanilla extract

### Strawberry Butter

1/2 cup (114 g) unsalted butter, at room temperature

1 tbsp (15 ml) water

6 strawberries, mashed with their juices (about 1/4 cup [60 ml] puree)

2 tbsp (30 ml) honey

This popovers recipe could not be easier: Preheat the oven to 400°F (200°C) and spray a 12-well muffin pan with nonstick olive oil spray. In a blender, combine the eggs, flour, milk, butter, salt and vanilla and blend for about 10 seconds on high speed. Once everything is well combined, pour equal amounts of the batter into each prepared well, filling each about three-quarters of the way full. Bake for 18 minutes, or until they are super puffy and golden brown. Once you take them out of the oven, they are going to deflate a lot; this is normal.

While the popovers bake, make the strawberry honey butter: In a stand mixer fitted with the paddle attachment or in a medium-sized bowl, using a hand mixer, whip together the butter and water for about 3 minutes, or until light and fluffy. Next, add your strawberries and whip for another 2 minutes or so, scraping down the sides as needed. Finally, add your honey and whip for another 1 to 2 minutes, or until fully combined. Store in an airtight container in the fridge when done using for this recipe.

Let the popovers cool in their pan for a few minutes, then transfer to a basket and serve warm with the strawberry honey butter.

**Notes**

1– *These can actually make pretty tasty breakfast "pancakes," too!*

## PAIRINGS

**Marinated Pork Tenderloin with Apple Chutney Made Sweet and Tangy with Balsamic Reduction (page 35)**

**Pumpkin Pasta with Andouille Sausage Made Special with Crème Fraîche and Brown Butter Walnut Sage Crumble (page 29)**

# EVERYDAY DECADENT DESSERTS

---

Desserts are important. They wrap up the meal with a nice, tasty bow. They bring comfort and happiness, so that's why they need to be absolutely delicious! The desserts you will find in this chapter are going to be exciting, decadent and, most of all, full of flavor. Experimenting with desserts is one of my favorite things to do, which is why you will find a lot of classic desserts with major twists in this book. Whether it's Elevated Maple Latte Crème Brûlée Made with Fresh Espresso (page 121), Thai Tea Panna Cotta with Mango Lassi Crema and Peanut Cashew Crumble (page 113) or Nostalgic PB+J Cheesecake Bites with Healthier Almond Flour Crust (page 118), there is definitely going to be something for everyone here, and hopefully a lot of new favorites will be made!

*Apple pie is a classic. A national treasure, if you will. Just because something is a classic, however, doesn't mean you can't mix it up a bit sometimes. These apple hand pies are stuffed to the brim with brown butter apples and creamy Brie cheese. The perfect combination of comfort and excitement, neatly wrapped up in flaky golden pie dough!*

# SIMPLE APPLE HAND PIES

## Stuffed with Brown Butter Apples and Chunks of Brie

**Prep time: 20 minutes** · **Cook time: 12 minutes** · **Servings: 6 hand pies**

2 tbsp (28 g) unsalted butter

2 cups (250 g) diced Granny Smith apple, cut into ¹/₂″ (1.3-cm) cubes

¹/₄ cup (56 g) light brown sugar

¹/₂ tsp ground cinnamon

¹/₈ tsp ground nutmeg

1 tsp fresh lemon juice

¹/₄ tsp salt

1 tbsp (8 g) cornstarch + 1 tbsp (15 ml) water, for a slurry

All-purpose flour, for dusting

2 (9″ [23-cm]) premade piecrusts

4 oz (113 g) diced Brie cheese, cut into ¹/₂″ (1.3-cm) cubes (see Notes)

1 large egg + 1 tbsp (15 ml) milk, for egg wash

**Notes**

1- *See more about how to brown butter on page 20.*

2- *You could leave out the Brie, if that's not your thing, or you can even replace it with some sharp white Cheddar for a bolder cheese flavor.*

Preheat the oven to 400°F (200°C). Line a large baking sheet with parchment paper. In a medium-sized saucepan over medium heat, melt the butter until browned (this will happen quickly). Add the apple cubes, brown sugar, cinnamon, nutmeg, lemon juice and salt to the browned butter. Bring to a boil, then lower the heat and cook down for 5 minutes, or until the apples are pierced easily with a fork.

In a small bowl, whisk together the cornstarch and water until it forms a slurry. Pour the cornstarch slurry into the apple mixture and allow it to thicken up for 2 to 3 minutes. Remove from the heat and spread on a dinner plate to let the apples cool quicker. You will want them to be room temperature when assembling the pies.

Once the apple filling has cooled, lightly dust a large, flat work surface with flour and roll out your piecrusts. Using a 4-inch (10-cm)-diameter circular cutter or a small glass bowl, cut 12 circles from the dough. Place six of the circles on your prepared baking sheet. In the center of each, place roughly 1 tablespoon (15 ml) of apple filling. Top with about five cubes of Brie (I like to smoosh them into the apples a little). Add 1 to 2 more teaspoons of the apple filling on top of the Brie to make sure it's tucked in nicely and the pies will be full.

In a small bowl, whisk together the egg and milk. Brush some of the egg wash around the outer edge of each the dough circle holding the filling; set the rest of the egg wash aside. Carefully place one of the remaining dough circles over the top of the filling and press down on the edges with your finger to seal it. Using the prongs of a fork, press the edges together to seal them completely, going all the way around. Using a sharp knife, make at least two 1-inch (2.5-cm) slits on the top of the pie. Repeat until you have made double-crust pies, then put them, baking sheet and all, in the freezer to chill for 10 minutes.

Next, remove the baking sheet from the freezer and lightly brush the remaining egg wash lightly over the top of all the pies. Bake for 12 to 14 minutes, or until the pies are golden brown. Remove from the oven and let cool for 10 minutes before serving. Serve warm by themselves or with vanilla ice cream!

*There's nothing better than warm chocolate chip cookies, am I right? Wrong. Let's elevate this classic with a couple of extra-easy steps: First, we brown the butter, giving it a crazy-delicious nuttiness. Next, we add the miso, which adds a huge umami pop of flavor. Now, let's try that again: There's nothing better than warm chocolate chip cookies with miso brown butter, right? Right!*

# EPIC SMALL-BATCH CHOCOLATE CHIP COOKIES

## Made Bakery Worthy with Miso Brown Butter

**Prep time: 15 minutes · Cook time: 12 minutes · Servings: 10 to 12 cookies**

1/2 cup (114 g) unsalted butter
1 cup (125 g) all-purpose flour
1/2 tsp salt
1/2 tsp instant espresso powder
1/4 tsp baking powder
1/4 tsp baking soda
1 tbsp (16 g) brown rice miso paste or white miso paste
2/3 cup (145 g) light brown sugar
1/4 cup (50 g) granulated sugar
1 large egg
1 tsp vanilla extract
1 cup (170 g) chocolate chips
Pinch of salt

### PAIRINGS

**Pumpkin Pasta with Andouille Sausage Made Special with Crème Fraîche and Brown Butter Walnut Sage Crumble (page 29)**

**Everyday Buttermilk Drop Biscuits with Cheddar and Roasted Garlic (page 86)**

Preheat the oven to 350°F (180°C). Line two baking sheets with parchment paper. One of the special parts of this recipe is browned butter. Brown the butter by melting it in a small saucepan over low heat until browned, which will take around 8 minutes.

While the butter browns, in a medium-sized bowl, mix together the flour, salt, espresso powder, baking powder and baking soda and set aside.

Once the butter has browned, pour it into a small bowl and add your miso paste to it, stirring well to combine. This is where the magic happens. In a large bowl, stir together your brown sugar, granulated sugar and the brown butter mixture. Add the egg and vanilla, then beat with a hand mixer for 2 minutes until it turns light gold and fluffy. Add your flour mixture and mix until fully incorporated; try not to overmix or the cookies will get too hard once baked.

Fold in the chocolate chips, then let the dough chill in the fridge for 30 minutes. Once the dough has chilled, scoop out around 2 tablespoons (30 ml) of dough and roll into a ball. Place the balls about 2 inches (5 cm) apart on the prepared baking sheet. Bake for 11 to 12 minutes, or until they start to brown.

Remove from the oven and allow to cool on the baking sheet for 5 minutes. Garnish with salt flakes. Transfer to a cooling rack and let cool. Store in an airtight container on the counter for up to 2 weeks.

### Notes

1- *See more about how to brown butter on page 20.*

*There is nothing more impressive than pavlova. It's like an edible work of art. You can put almost any fruit on top of one and it will turn out delicious. You normally see bright berries and springlike flavor combinations when it comes to pavlovas, so I wanted to make one that would be perfect for fall and winter. This is my apple pie pavlova! The warm spice of cinnamon in the meringue and the spiced apples sautéed in brown butter will make you and your taste buds feel nice and cozy.*

# APPROACHABLE MINI CINNAMON PAVLOVAS

## Elevated with Brown Butter Caramelized Apples

**Prep time: 20 minutes · Cook time: 1 hour · Servings: 6 pavlovas**

### Pavlovas

½ cup (120 ml) egg whites (from about 4 eggs), at room temperature
1 cup (200 g) granulated sugar
1½ tsp (4 g) cornstarch
1 tsp fresh lemon juice
¼ tsp vanilla extract
½ tsp ground cinnamon

### Brown Butter Caramelized Apples

3 tbsp (43 g) unsalted butter
2 cups (240 g) finely diced apples (from about 2 large apples)
⅓ cup (75 g) light brown sugar
½ tsp ground cinnamon
Pinch of salt

The most important first step is to gather all your ingredients and carefully read through the entire recipe so you will be prepared for each step as it comes. That has given me the most success while making pavlovas.

Make the pavlovas: Preheat the oven to 225°F (100°C) and line a large baking sheet with parchment paper. Place the egg whites in an absolutely clean (wipe down the bowl and whisk attachment with lemon juice before starting) stainless-steel or glass bowl of a stand mixer fitted with the whisk attachment. Beat the egg whites on high speed for 1 minute. Slowly add the granulated sugar, about 1 tablespoon (13 g) every 30 seconds, until all the sugar is incorporated. Beat until smooth and stiff peaks form and everything is nice and glossy. Fold in the cornstarch, lemon juice, vanilla and cinnamon until well incorporated.

Using a spoon or spatula, make six small mounds of meringue, each about 4 inches (10 cm) in diameter, about 3 inches (7.5 cm) apart, on your prepared baking sheet. Smooth them around the outside and create a small dip at the top, making them resemble nests. Bake for 1 hour and then turn off the oven, but leave them in and *do not open the door.* The pavlovas need to cool down slowly or they will crack.

Make the apple mixture while the pavlovas cool: In a large skillet, melt the butter until browned. This will only take a couple of minutes and makes a *huge* difference in flavor. Once it's browned, add the apples, brown sugar, cinnamon and salt. Cook for around 10 more minutes, stirring occasionally, until they are nice and tender. Remove from the heat and allow to cool almost completely before assembling,

(continued)

# APPROACHABLE MINI CINNAMON PAVLOVAS (continued)

### Whipped Cream

1 cup (240 ml) heavy cream

1 tbsp (8 g) powdered sugar, plus more for serving

1 tsp vanilla extract

While the apples cool, make the whipped cream: In a large bowl, using a hand mixer or a stand mixer fitted with the whisk attachment, combine the cream, powdered sugar and vanilla and whip for 4 to 5 minutes, or until stiff peaks form.

When everything is done, assemble the pavlovas by topping each with a dollop of the whipped cream and then about a tablespoon (7 g) or a little more of the apples. Sprinkle them with powdered sugar, if desired, and serve.

## PAIRINGS

**Weeknight Steak Tips with Miso Garlic Butter (page 39)**

**Simple Loaded and Smashed Potatoes with Hot Honey Crème Fraîche Drizzle (page 90)**

*Thai tea is one of my all-time favorite flavors. Ever since I tried it, I have loved it and have made it my life's mission to infuse it into as many desserts as possible. It gives this panna cotta a beautiful, mild spiced flavor and pairs perfectly with the mango lassi crema and peanut cashew crumble. This dish has it all. It's spicy (think: cardamom, cinnamon and cloves), sweet, creamy and crunchy!*

# THAI TEA PANNA COTTA

## with Mango Lassi Crema and Peanut Cashew Crumble

**Prep time: 20 minutes** · **Cook time: 20 minutes** · **Cool time: 4 hours** · **Servings: 6**

### Thai Tea Panna Cotta

1³/₄ cups (420 ml) whole milk, divided
1 cinnamon stick
¹/₄ tsp ground cardamom
4 Thai tea bags, or 3 tbsp (18 g) loose tea
1 tbsp (7 g) unflavored gelatin
¹/₃ cup (67 g) granulated sugar
1¹/₂ cups (360 ml) heavy cream
1 tsp vanilla extract, or 1 vanilla bean pod
Pinch of salt

### Peanut Cashew Crumble

¹/₂ cup (75 g) peanuts
¹/₃ cup (47 g) cashews
¹/₂ cup (42 g) unsweetened coconut flakes
2 tbsp (16 g) sesame seeds
1 tbsp (15 ml) coconut oil
2 tbsp (30 ml) pure maple syrup
¹/₄ tsp ground cardamom
¹/₂ tsp cinnamon

Make the panna cotta: In a medium-sized saucepan, bring 1 cup (240 ml) of the milk to a simmer over medium-low heat. Remove from the heat, add the cinnamon stick, cardamom and tea, then let steep for 15 minutes. Strain everything out and save the milk for later in a small glass bowl. Wash the saucepan for the next step.

Into the washed saucepan, pour the remaining ³/₄ cup (175 ml) of milk and then sprinkle the gelatin on top. Let it bloom for 5 minutes undisturbed and then place over low heat. Add the Thai tea-infused milk and your sugar. Heat for 2 minutes, stirring constantly so the sugar melts. Once the sugar is melted, remove from the heat add your cream, vanilla and salt. Mix well for another 2 to 3 minutes and then strain. I like to strain this again because that gets out leftover spices and also undissolved gelatin, so we have a nice and smooth panna cotta base. Now, go ahead and pour your liquid equally into six dishes (see Notes). I like to set the dishes on a baking sheet so it's easier and flatter to carry. Place them, covered, in the fridge for at least 4 hours or overnight.

When you are ready to serve your panna cotta, make the peanut cashew crumble: Preheat the oven to 350°F (180°C) and line a large baking sheet with parchment paper. In a food processor, pulse the peanuts and cashews until fine but still crumbly. Transfer the nuts to a medium-sized glass bowl and then add the coconut flakes, sesame seeds, coconut oil, maple syrup, cardamom and cinnamon. Mix until well combined, then transfer to the prepared baking sheet and spread out until even. Bake for 30 minutes, stirring at the 15-minute point.

(continued)

# THAI TEA PANNA COTTA
## (continued)

**Mango Lassi Crema**

1 cup (175 g) peeled and diced mango, plus more for serving

3/4 cup (173 g) plain yogurt

1/4 cup (60 ml) sweetened condensed milk

Now, for the mango lassi! This is super easy: In a blender, combine the mango, yogurt and sweetened condensed milk and blend until smooth. Once this is done, you can serve your panna cotta by turning it out onto a plate, covering it with the mango lassi and sprinkling the peanut cashew crumble on top. Serve with the extra diced mango on the side.

## PAIRINGS

**Easy Miso Salmon Bite Bowl with Creamy Sriracha Sauce (page 47)**

**Easy Deviled Eggs Made Restaurant Worthy by Marinating in Soy Sauce with a Creamy Sriracha Filling (page 67)**

**Notes**

1- *You are going to want to prep your bowl or molds for this first. This recipe will make six 4-ounce (120-ml) panna cottas. You can use all kinds of things to serve panna cotta, the most popular being a small ramekin. I actually used a cool mold I found on Amazon that helped them pop out easier, but you don't even have to pop them out at all! You can serve them right in a jar, dish or glass—basically whatever you decide you want to use or have on hand. If you do want to pop them out of the container, though, you will need to very lightly oil the inside of the dish. I put some olive or avocado oil on a paper towel and rubbed it around the inside of the dish I used and it worked perfectly.*

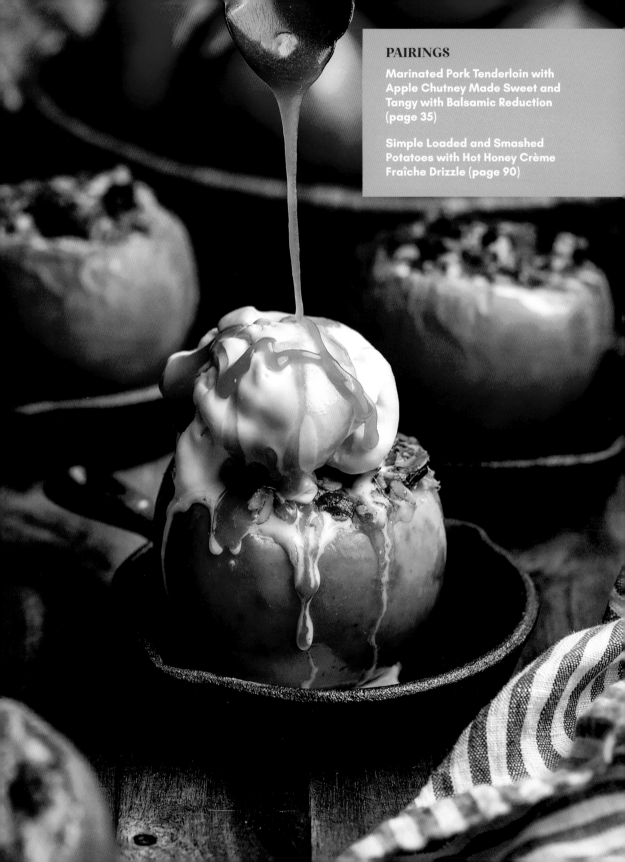

**PAIRINGS**

**Marinated Pork Tenderloin with
Apple Chutney Made Sweet and
Tangy with Balsamic Reduction
(page 35)**

**Simple Loaded and Smashed
Potatoes with Hot Honey Crème
Fraîche Drizzle (page 90)**

*You know what always makes me happy? An easy dessert. Sometimes, desserts can just be really intense and it almost isn't even worth it, you know what I mean? Well, this is not one of those desserts! These stuffed apples couldn't be easier; even the caramel sauce is quick and easy. The apples are stuffed with a sweet filling like most, but I've added my secret weapon, Brie, to shake this recipe up a bit. You've never had baked apples like this one; that's a promise.*

# EASY STUFFED BAKED APPLES

## Made Restaurant Worthy with Brie and a Quick Caramel Sauce

**Prep time: 10 minutes** · **Cook time: 45 minutes** · **Servings: 4**

### Baked Apples

$^1/_2$ cup (45 g) old-fashioned oats

$^1/_2$ cup (50 g) pecans

$^1/_4$ cup (25 g) fresh cranberries

$^1/_4$ cup (56 g) light brown sugar

5 tbsp (71 g) unsalted butter, melted

$^1/_4$ tsp salt

8 oz (125 g) Brie cheese, small diced

4 apples, such as Honeycrisp, Fuji or Granny Smith (see Notes)

$^1/_2$ cup (120 ml) warm water (100 to 110°F)

Ice cream, to serve

### Quick Caramel Sauce

$^1/_4$ cup (57 g) unsalted butter

$^3/_4$ cup (169 g) light brown sugar

$^1/_4$ cup (60 ml) heavy cream

Fill and bake the apples: Preheat the oven to 375°F (190°C). In a medium-sized bowl, mix together your oats, pecans, cranberries, brown sugar, melted butter, salt and Brie chunks until well combined. Prepare the apples by cutting the top off and then scooping out the center to remove the core as well as a little more of the inside.

Fill each apple pretty full with about $^1/_2$ cup (120 ml) of filling, pushing the stuffing in a little along the way to make sure each center is nice and full. Place the apples in a glass baking dish that fits them all comfortably. Pour the warm water around the apples and bake for 40 to 45 minutes, or until the apples are tender.

While the apples bake, make the caramel sauce: In a small saucepan, melt the butter, and then add the brown sugar and cream. Whisk vigorously until the brown sugar is melted and everything is smooth. Remove from the heat, let cool, then store in the fridge in an airtight glass container.

Once the apples are tender, remove from the oven and allow to cool partially. Top with a scoop of ice cream and drizzle your caramel sauce all over the top.

**Notes**

1- *Not all apples are created equal—for baking, that is! The best apples to use for baking are Granny Smith, Honeycrisp, Rome Beauty, Braeburn, Pink Lady and Golden Delicious.*

2- *Use this caramel sauce on everything. You can even use it in your coffee!*

*Take a trip down memory lane with me and these bites! They are super simple to make, crazy light and fluffy and make you feel like a kid again. The peanut butter and raspberry jam are elevated to a whole new flavor level when added to cheesecake, not to mention added on top of the slightly spiced crumble bottom, supplying a much-needed spice kick to this classic combo. Creamier and sweeter than you ever imagined, these are something you can actually enjoy with your kids, and that's always a plus!*

# NOSTALGIC PB+J CHEESECAKE BITES

## with Healthier Almond Flour Crust

**Prep time: 10 minutes • Cook time: 35 minutes • Servings: 12 cheesecake bites**

### Crust

Olive oil cooking spray

1 cup (100 g) almond flour

2 tbsp (16 g) powdered sugar

$^1/_2$ tsp ground cinnamon

$^1/_4$ cup (57 g) unsalted butter, melted

### Filling

12 oz (340 g) cream cheese, at room temperature

$^3/_4$ cup (90 g) powdered sugar

2 large eggs

$^1/_4$ cup (64 g) peanut butter

1 tsp vanilla extract

$^1/_2$ tsp salt

$^1/_4$ cup (80 g) raspberry jelly

You and your whole family are going to *love* this recipe! Let's get started by making the crust: Preheat the oven to 300°F (150°C). Spray a 12-well muffin pan with cooking spray. In a medium-sized bowl, combine the almond flour, powdered sugar and cinnamon, then add the melted butter and mix until incorporated. Divide equally among the prepared muffin cups. Press the crust down into the bottom of each cup and slightly up the sides until about $^1/_4$ inch (6 mm) thick and tightly pressed. Bake for 10 to 15 minutes, or until browned, and then remove from the oven. Let cool in the pan for 10 minutes while you make the filling. Leave the oven on.

To make the filling, place the cream cheese in a large bowl and beat until smooth. Add the powdered sugar, eggs, peanut butter, vanilla and salt and continue to beat briefly until fully combined. Distribute the filling equally among the crusts, then place 1 teaspoon of jelly on top of each portion of filling. Using a toothpick, swirl the jelly around to incorporate and create a swirl pattern on top. This would be a really fun part for the kids to do if you are making this as a family activity!

Return the pan to the oven and bake for 25 minutes, or until set. You can tell because the filling will only slightly jiggle when you move the pan. Once set, remove from the oven and let cool for at least 30 minutes in the pan before removing.

## PAIRINGS

**Loaded Potato and Leek Soup Elevated with Smoky Cheddar, Crispy Pancetta and Crème Fraîche (page 56)**

**Approachable Autumn Squash Soup with Andouille Sausage, Cheddar and Coconut Milk (page 64)**

*This crème brûlée is unlike any you've ever had. It is inspired by a maple latte that I've never had but it just sounded good. Doesn't this sound good? Well, good news, it tastes amazing! The coffee flavor isn't overwhelming, and neither is the maple. They are just happily coexisting in a classic dessert that we all know and love!*

# ELEVATED MAPLE LATTE CRÈME BRÛLÉE

## Made with Fresh Espresso

**Prep time: 10 minutes · Cook time: 40 minutes · Cool time: 2 hours · Servings: 4**

2 quarts (1.9 L) water
2¼ cups (540 ml) heavy cream
5 large egg yolks
⅓ cup (67 g) granulated sugar, plus more for topping
⅛ tsp salt
½ tsp vanilla extract
¼ tsp maple extract
1 shot prepared espresso (about 3 tbsp [45 ml]; see Notes)

### PAIRINGS

**Weeknight Steak Tips with Miso Garlic Butter (page 39)**

**Classic Wedge Salad with Blue Cheese Dressing and Cured Egg Yolk (page 98)**

Preheat the oven to 325°F (170°C). Place four 6-ounce (175-ml) ramekins in a large baking dish. Bring the water to a boil.

In a small saucepan over medium-low heat, heat the cream until steaming (do not boil).

Meanwhile, place your egg yolks in a large bowl, sprinkle the sugar over them and whisk together until light in color. Once the cream is heated, remove the pan from the heat, add the salt, vanilla, maple extract and espresso, and then temper the egg mixture by slowly pouring a skinny stream of the cream mixture into the bowl while whisking. Once about ¼ cup (60 ml) has been added, you can go ahead and add the rest of the cream mixture to the egg mixture. Stir well until combined.

Pour an equal amount of this mixture into each of the ramekins. Then, pour the boiling water into the baking dish halfway up the outside of the ramekins. Bake for 40 minutes, or until the centers are stable but still jiggly. Remove from the oven, let cool completely on the counter and place in the refrigerator to cool completely, at least 30 minutes.

Remove from the fridge and sprinkle a layer of sugar over the top. I like to sprinkle the sugar and then dump the excess off by turning the ramekin upside down over the sink. You don't want too much sugar or it will burn and have a bad taste. Broil in the oven for 2 to 3 minutes (watch carefully), or until sugar is melted and browned, or use a kitchen torch to brown the top.

### Notes

1- *If you don't have espresso, you can use 3 tablespoons (45 ml) of strongly brewed coffee instead.*

*This recipe is inspired by one of my favorite childhood cakes. It was an Easter dessert we always had, with lemon curd filling and seven-minute frosting. I just had to re-create it for my cookbook, so here we are! Fluffy yellow box cake (better than homemade, in my opinion), blood orange custard filling and a marshmallow-y meringue frosting to give all your taste buds a sunny memory from me and my childhood.*

# BLOOD ORANGE CUSTARD LAYER CAKE

Made Easy with Box Cake and Quick Marshmallow Meringue Frosting

**Prep time: 10 minutes · Cook time: 20 minutes · Cool time: 2 hours · Servings: 10**

1 (15.25-oz [433-g]) box yellow cake mix

Custard
²/₃ cup (133 g) granulated sugar
2 tbsp (16 g) cornstarch
¹/₈ tsp salt
2 tsp (4 g) grated orange zest
²/₃ cup (160 ml) blood orange juice
2 tbsp (30 ml) fresh lemon juice
4 large egg yolks
1 large egg
¹/₄ cup (57 g) unsalted butter, diced

Make the cake according to the package instructions, then make the custard; they both need to be completely cool before assembly.

To make the custard, in a medium-sized saucepan, whisk together the sugar, cornstarch and salt. Stir in the orange zest, orange juice and lemon juice. Bring to a boil over medium heat, stirring constantly, and let boil for about 1 minute. Remove from the heat.

In a medium-sized glass bowl, whisk the egg yolks and whole egg until well blended. We are going to temper the eggs by slowly adding ¹/₄ cup (60 ml) of the boiled juice mixture, in a slow stream, to the eggs while whisking constantly. This makes sure the eggs don't cook and scramble in the heat. Once all of the juice mixture is added to the eggs, add the egg mixture to the pot and place back on the stove over medium-low heat. Whisk vigorously for around 4 minutes, or until the mixture thickens. Remove from the heat and add the diced butter. Stir until combined and then pour into a heatproof glass bowl. Cover the custard with a plastic wrap touching it (to prevent a skin from forming) and chill in the fridge for at least 2 hours.

(continued)

# BLOOD ORANGE CUSTARD LAYER CAKE (continued)

**Marshmallow Meringue Frosting**

4 large egg whites
1 cup (200 g) granulated sugar
$^1/_2$ tsp cream of tartar
1 tsp vanilla extract

Once the custard and cake are cool, make the frosting: Using the double boiler method, in a medium-sized heatproof glass bowl, combine the egg whites, sugar and cream of tartar. Bring a few inches (about 5 cm) of water to a boil in a small saucepan and place the bowl atop the saucepan (the water saucepan should be low enough to not touch the bowl). Stir and heat the egg mixture until the sugar is well incorporated (you can test this by rubbing a little bit between your fingers and seeing whether it's still grainy, but be careful; it will be hot), and then remove from the heat, stir in the vanilla and transfer to the bowl of a stand mixer fitted with the whisk attachment. Beat on high speed for about 5 minutes, or until stiff glossy peaks form.

Assembly time! Place a nice, thick layer of custard between the two cake layers. You can even split the layers in half to create a total of four layers, which is a little tricky but will make a taller, fancier-looking cake. Once the cake is assembled with the custard filling, spread the meringue frosting all over the cake, then lightly brown with a kitchen torch.

## PAIRINGS

**Simple Summer Fettuccine Made Restaurant Worthy with Cherry Tomato Garlic Confit Sauce (page 25)**

**Classic Wedge Salad with Blue Cheese Dressing and Cured Egg Yolk (page 98)**

### Notes

1– *The real star of this show is the blood orange custard, but if you have a favorite yellow cake recipe, go for it! The only thing you need to do if you substitute that is to make it in two 9-inch (23-cm) round pans.*

2– *You can also make this into filled cupcakes (as shown in the photo on the left page). All you need to do differently is follow the directions on the box for cupcakes; mine took 18 minutes to bake. Then, you will just remove part of the center of each cupcake (I use a 1-inch [2.5-cm] round cookie cutter) and fill with the custard. Pipe the meringue frosting on top of each cupcake and then lightly torch.*

*This is going to become your go to snacking cake. It gets easier and easier to make each time, too. I know you probably hear their cake is the "best ever" from a lot from people when they bake a cake, but this cake is good, y'all. The chai spice adds a spicy warmth; the brown sugar butter mixture seeps into the cake, making it incredibly moist and cara-mel-y; and the buttermilk makes it extra fluffy. You will be hard pressed to find someone who doesn't end up absolutely loving this cake; that's a promise.*

# BEST EVER APPLE UPSIDE-DOWN CAKE

## with Buttermilk and Chai Spice

**Prep time: 15 hours** · **Cook time: 45 minutes** · **Servings: 8 to 10**

### Topping

$^1/_2$ cup (114 g) unsalted butter
$^1/_2$ cup (113 g) dark brown sugar
$^1/_4$ tsp vanilla extract
$^1/_4$ tsp chai spice mix (see page 18)
2 apples, peeled, cored and sliced thinly (see Notes)

### Cake Batter

1$^1/_3$ cups (167 g) all-purpose flour
$^3/_4$ tsp baking powder
$^1/_4$ tsp baking soda
$^1/_2$ tsp salt
1 tsp chai spice mix (see page 18)
6 tbsp (85 g) unsalted butter, at room temperature
$^1/_2$ cup (100 g) granulated sugar
$^1/_4$ cup (56 g) dark brown sugar
1 large egg
1 tsp vanilla extract
$^2/_3$ cup (160 ml) buttermilk

### Notes

*1- You can switch up the fruit you use, but I think apple is the best!*

Preheat the oven to 350°F (180°C). You will need an ungreased 9-inch (23-cm) round cake pan or pie pan for this cake.

Make the topping: In a medium-sized saucepan, melt the butter over medium-high heat. Add the brown sugar and mix until well combined. Remove from the heat, add the vanilla and chai spice, then pour the mixture into the bottom of your cake pan. Arrange your apple slices in the pan in a circular pattern, starting on the outside and working your way in. Make sure they are close together so there is apple in every bite! Place the cake pan in the fridge to set the caramel apple topping while you make the cake batter.

Make the cake batter: In a medium-sized bowl, mix together the flour, baking powder, baking soda, salt and chai spice, then set aside. In the bowl of a stand mixer fitted with the paddle attachment, or a large bowl, using a hand mixer, beat the butter until fluffy, about 1 minute. Add the granulated and brown sugars and beat until fluffy and light in color, about 3 minutes. Add the egg and vanilla and beat until combined. Scrape down the sides and continue to mix for another minute or so. Next, you are going to add one-third of your flour mixture, followed by $^1/_3$ cup (80 ml) of the buttermilk. Repeat with half of the remaining flour mixture and the remaining $^1/_3$ cup of buttermilk, then finish it with the remaining flour mixture, making sure to scrape down the sides of the bowl every so often to make sure everything is incorporated. Take the cake pan out of the fridge and pour the cake batter evenly over the topping.

Bake at 350°F (180°C) for 40 to 45 minutes, or until golden brown and a toothpick inserted into the center comes out clean. Allow it to cool on a wire rack for 10 minutes. Then, run a knife around the edge of the cake and carefully flip it over onto another wire rack. Let cool for another 20 to 30 minutes, or until cool enough to eat.

**PAIRINGS**

**Everyday Chicken Skewers with Flavor-Popping Miso Marinade (page 40)**

**Easy Fondant Sweet Potatoes Elevated with Miso Maple Walnut Glaze (page 85)**

*This is not your average boring coffee cake. I know what you're thinking—crème fraîche in a coffee cake sounds weird—and I will admit it does sound weird. However, you are just going to have to trust me on this one, because it's about to blow your mind. It gives the cake an extra depth of richness and helps keep it nice and fluffy. This recipe is going to be on repeat at your house, and anyone who gets a slice is going to be singing your praises.*

# MAPLE COFFEE CAKE

### Elevated with Crème Fraîche

**Prep time: 15 minutes · Cook time: 40 minutes · Cool time: 10 minutes · Servings: 9 slices**

Nonstick olive oil spray, for pan

### Streusel
3/4 cup (90 g) all-purpose flour
2/3 cup (145 g) light brown sugar
6 tbsp (85 g) unsalted butter, cold, cut into small cubes
1 tsp ground cinnamon or chai spice mix (see page 18)
1/8 tsp salt

### Cake Batter
1 1/3 cups (167 g) all-purpose flour
1 tsp baking powder
1/4 tsp baking soda
1/4 tsp salt
1/2 cup (114 g) unsalted butter, at room temperature
1/2 cup (100 g) granulated sugar
1/4 cup (38 g) maple sugar or (56 g) light brown sugar
2 large eggs, at room temperature
2 tsp (10 ml) vanilla extract
1/4 tsp maple extract
1/2 cup (115 g) crème fraîche

### Drizzle
1/2 cup (60 g) powdered sugar
1 tbsp (15 ml) pure maple syrup

Preheat the oven to 350°F (180°C). Line an 8-inch (20-cm) square cake pan with parchment paper so it covers the bottom and then comes up the sides, making it easier to remove, then lightly spray with nonstick olive oil spray.

First, make the streusel: In a medium-sized bowl, combine the flour, brown sugar, cubed butter, cinnamon and salt, then crumble with a fork, pastry cutter or your fingers until well mixed and crumbly.

Now, make the cake batter: In a medium-sized bowl, stir together the flour, baking powder, baking soda and salt, then set aside. In a stand mixer fitted with the paddle attachment, or a large bowl, using a hand mixer, beat together your butter, granulated sugar and maple sugar on medium-high speed for about 3 minutes, or until light colored and fluffy. Add the eggs, one at a time, beating after each addition, and then the vanilla and maple extracts. Beat in the crème fraîche, then add the flour mixture slowly until *just* combined. The mixture will be very thick.

Spread half of the batter on the bottom of your prepared cake pan. Sprinkle half of the streusel mixture evenly over the batter, then carefully spread the rest of the batter on top of that. This will be slightly difficult because of how thick the batter is, but it's nothing you can't do! Just put most of the batter in the center of the pan, go slowly and spread outward. Sprinkle the rest of the streusel evenly on top, covering the batter. Bake for 40 minutes, or until a toothpick inserted into the center comes out clean.

While the cake bakes, make the drizzle: In a small bowl, mix together the powdered sugar and maple syrup until well combined. Once the cake is out of the oven, let cool for 10 minutes in the pan and then pour drizzle all over!

*Get ready to swoon over this tart, because it is decadent. If you looked up the word "decadent" in the dictionary, a picture of this tart would be there. I mean, we start with a crust of Oreos, pretty much the best way to begin anything. Then there's a layer of homemade raspberry jam topped with the smoothest, creamiest and most flavorful ganache layer you've ever had. This is because the ganache has a super special and elevated twist that makes it more special than any other ganache tart you've ever had: red wine! A chocolate and wine lover's dream.*

# EXPLOSIVE RED WINE GANACHE TART

## with Raspberry Jam Layer and Chocolate Crust

**Prep time: 45 minutes** · **Cool time: 4 hours** · **Servings: 6**

### Jam

1¹/₂ cups (188 g) fresh raspberries
1 tbsp (15 ml) fresh lemon juice
2 tbsp (30 ml) pure maple syrup
2 tbsp (20 g) chia seeds

### Crust

32 chocolate sandwich cookies (I prefer Oreos)
6 tbsp (85 g) unsalted butter, melted

Let's make our homemade jam first, so it has time to cool. This couldn't be easier! In a small saucepan, combine the raspberries, lemon juice, maple syrup and chia seeds. Mash the raspberries a little to help incorporate them. Place over medium-high heat and let reduce for about 10 minutes, or until mashed and reduced to a jam consistency. Remove from the heat and transfer to an airtight container, without its lid, and allow to cool. If not using immediately, cover and place in the fridge. Allow to come to room temperature or cool completely before adding to the tart.

Preheat the oven to 350°F (180°C).

I decided to use Oreos for the crust because they are, in my opinion, the best chocolate cookie that exists. Plus, they have the cream filling inside, which definitely adds to this crust. To make the crust, pulse the entire cookies in a food processor until very fine. Pour in the melted butter and pulse some more until the cookie crumble is moist and it stays together when you press it between your fingers. Pour this mixture into a 9-inch (23-cm) round tart pan and press down, using the bottom of a measuring cup, and up the side, using your fingers. Make sure it's nice and tight! Bake for 7 minutes to make sure it stays together.

After the jam is cool, spread it over the crust in a thin layer and then place the pan in the freezer for 30 minutes to solidify it before you pour the hot ganache on top.

(continued)

# EXPLOSIVE RED WINE GANACHE TART (continued)

### Ganache

6 oz (170 g) bittersweet chocolate, chopped finely

6 oz (170 g) milk chocolate, chopped finely

1/4 cup (60 ml) red wine (see Notes)

3/4 cup (180 ml) heavy cream

1/4 cup (1/2 stick/57 g) unsalted butter

1 tsp vanilla extract

Pinch of salt

### Toppings

Fresh fruit

Crushed Pistachios

## PAIRINGS

**Pumpkin Pasta with Andouille Sausage Made Special with Crème Fraîche and Brown Butter Walnut Sage Crumble (page 29)**

**Southern Comfort Gouda Grit Cakes Topped with Cherry Tomato Garlic Confit (page 78)**

While the tart in the freezer, make the ganache: In a medium-sized heatproof bowl, combine the finely chopped chocolate and my not-so-secret but definitely special ingredient: red wine. In a medium-sized saucepan, combine the cream and butter and heat over medium-low heat until just barely boiling. Remove from the heat, then add the vanilla and salt. Pour this mixture over the chocolate mixture and let it sit for 1 minute before stirring. Once the chocolate and cream mixtures are completely combined, remove the tart from the freezer and pour the ganache evenly on top of the jam layer in the tart.

Store the tart in the fridge (not the freezer) for at least 2 hours before serving. I like to wait 4 hours, this way I know that when I remove it from the tart pan it will stay together, and I top mine with fresh fruit and crushed pistachios. Enjoy!

**Notes**

1- *When cooking with wine, I follow the rule that I only cook with wine that I enjoy drinking. Nothing is different for this recipe, so use some red wine you wouldn't mind also having a glass of while you make this delicious tart!*

2- *You can get really fancy with the topping or you can keep it super simple, totally up to you and your imagination. Try a glazed fruit topping, crushed nuts, sea salt or even caramel.*

*In my humble opinion, there aren't many things better than the pear and blue cheese pairing. This galette brings that powerful flavor combination to a whole new level by layering it on top of a flaky pie dough, brushing the pears with honey, then ending with a sprinkle of a brown butter crispy sage and walnut crumble for an additional salty crunch. Pretty much perfection. Also, I'm pretty sure this is one of, if not the easiest, recipes to make in this entire cookbook! Why? Because of my secret ingredient: premade pie dough! I mean, if you want to make your own pie dough from scratch, go for it. But for me, personally, why waste the time when the premade doughs are freaking delicious and ready to go?*

# EASIEST EVER BLUE CHEESE PEAR GALETTE

## with Brown Butter Sage Walnut Crumble

**Prep time: 10 minutes · Cook time: 40 minutes · Servings: 8**

### Blue Cheese Pear Galette

1 premade (9" [23-cm]) piecrust, at room temperature

4 Bosc pears

3 tbsp (24 g) crumbled blue cheese

2 tbsp (25 g) whipped cream cheese

1 large egg + 1 tsp water, for egg wash

2 tbsp (30 ml) honey

Make the galette: Preheat the oven to 425°F (220°C) and line a large baking sheet with parchment paper. Roll out your room-temperature piecrust and place in the center of the prepared baking sheet.

Prep your pears by slicing in half, scooping out the center seeds and then thinly slicing while keeping their shape. In a medium-sized bowl, mix together your blue cheese and whipped cream cheese until well combined. Spread this around the center of the pie crust, leaving a 2- to 3-inch (5- to 7.5-cm) bare border around the outside. Lay your pears on top of the cheese spread, fit nice and snug together, then slowly fold the border of the piecrust up and slightly over the pears. Leave the entire center exposed, but it's almost as if you're tucking the pears in on the outside. Place the galette in the freezer to chill for about 10 minutes, just to solidify the dough and filing a little before baking.

While the galette is in the freezer, make an egg wash: In a small bowl, whisk together the egg and water. When you remove the galette from the freezer, brush the egg wash on the exposed outer edge of the dough. Bake for 30 to 40 minutes, or until the dough turns golden brown.

(continued)

# EASIEST EVER BLUE CHEESE PEAR GALETTE (continued)

## Sage Walnut Crumble

2 tbsp (28 g) unsalted butter
6 sage leaves, plus more for garnish
1/2 cup (50 g) walnuts
2 tsp (10 g) light brown sugar
1/2 tsp salt

When the pie bakes, make your crumble: You'll see this crumble a lot throughout my cookbook because it is the ultimate added crunch we all crave. Sweet, salty, nutty and a little herby. First, in a medium-sized skillet, melt the butter over medium heat. Once it starts to foam and brown, add your sage leaves and allow them to crisp up (should take less than 3 minutes). Remove the sage leaves and place them on a paper towel–covered plate. Add the walnuts to the pan and toast for about 5 minutes, then transfer them to a small bowl. Crumble the sage leaves into the bowl, then add the brown sugar and salt. Mix well and set aside.

Once your galette looks nice and browned, remove from the oven and brush the pears with the honey, then sprinkle with the brown butter sage walnut crumble and garnish with sage leaves and serve warm.

## PAIRINGS

Loaded Potato and Leek Soup Elevated with Smoky Cheddar, Crispy Pancetta and Crème Fraîche (page 56)

Tastiest Sourdough Bruschetta Elevated with Flavorful Herb Oil and Topped with Crispy Capers (page 71)

### Notes

1- *This galette tastes amazing with a scoop of vanilla ice cream. Give it a shot; you won't regret it.*

2- *If you like the idea of this dessert, but don't like blue cheese, try it with goat cheese instead.*

# About the Author

**Jenny Hurley** is a food photographer and videographer, as well as the founder and recipe developer of the flavor-forward food blog Sunny with Shadows. Food is what makes Jenny the most happy, and the tastier, the better. She loves to try new foods and dreams of eating at every Michelin-starred restaurant out there. Having always been passionate about photography, it was only a matter of time before she used the mediums of photography, videography and explosive flavor combinations to bring food to life.

Jenny is a mom to one little boy who constantly inspires her and pushes her to do more without even knowing it, and a wife to a loving husband who always supports her, no matter what. She also has two dogs and two cats that are constantly bothering her, but she still loves them anyway. In her spare time, she loves painting murals on the walls of different rooms in her house and designing interesting and fun spaces for her family to live in.

# Acknowledgments

I'd like to start by thanking the Page Street Publishing team, especially Aïcha, for being so awesome. You are all so kind and have made this whole process exciting and as smooth as possible.

I'd like to thank my mom, who taught me comfort through the food she made and for just always having dinner on the table, no matter what. I still request certain recipes from her that I love to this day, and she makes them. She's my go-to whenever I have a cooking issue, need a certain sized pan, need help watching my kid so I can work or pretty much anything else you can think of. She also does my taxes because she's a CPA and that rocks.

I'd like to thank my dad, who taught me some of the finer things in the food world at a young age. I don't know a lot of other kids who were eating garlic-stuffed olives and escargot at 10 years old. Whether it is perfecting the cooking method of Peking duck at home or going out to fancy restaurants, he is still always on the hunt for the finest and most interesting foods he can find.

I'd like to thank my sister, because I literally didn't know this job existed until she did it. She gave me my first food photography gig and that pretty much set me on the path I'm on today.

I need to thank my kid, because he changed me forever. He's made me who I am today, and he doesn't even know it. I love you more than anything, kid.

I'd most of all like to thank my husband. He has been, and always is, incredibly supportive in whatever I want to do. He just knows I can do it, even when I'm overthinking everything. I couldn't do any of it without him.

Lastly, I have to thank all of you, my followers, my friends, who have supported me and got me where I am today in my career. It is the most amazing feeling to have people you don't even know trust you enough to make your recipe in the first place—but to believe in you so much that they buy your cookbook? Now, that's amazing. Thank you.

# Index